PRAISE FOR

new day
revolution

"Most think that change emanates from BIG—big money, big ideas, and big people. What Sam and Stephen have realized, and what you can learn from *New Day Revolution*, is that MOST change comes through the decisions we make in our everyday lives. The kind of friend, citizen, consumer you are CAN change the world, much more than charity ever can. *New Day Revolution* is a manifesto for a new life—yours."

ROBERT EGGER
PRESIDENT, DC CENTRAL KITCHEN AND AUTHOR OF *BEGGING FOR CHANGE*

"*New Day Revolution* is a compelling call for us all to dip our toes in the waters of socially and environmentally conscious and caring action. The water level rises, and before long we're all swimming in a peaceful world."

GABE DIXON
SINGER/SONGWRITER, THE GABE DIXON BAND

"William Faulkner wrote, 'The man who removes a mountain begins by carrying away small stones.' *New Day Revolution* by Sam Davidson and Stephen Moseley was like discovering how to transform the world one stone at a time, one day at a time, one practical step at a time. It's not novel to stir people up over the notion of changing the world, but what is profoundly unique about Davidson and Moseley's message is that it offers a doable guide for making a difference along the everyday paths of life where we live our lives. It's been a while since I've read a book that so powerfully challenged me toward a more hopeful way of living, and a book I truly loved and enjoyed reading."

JIM PALMER
AUTHOR OF *DIVINE NOBODIES: SHEDDING RELIGION TO FIND GOD (AND THE UNLIKELY PEOPLE WHO HELP YOU)* AND *WIDE OPEN SPACES: BEYOND PAINT-BY-NUMBER CHRISTIANITY*

"This sunny, neighborly book is a good way to get in sync with the planet. Contrary to what Kermit told us on Sesame Street, it's easy being green. The authors make it cool and fun to focus on the little things in life that add up to make a better world."

JIM COOPER
U.S. CONGRESSMAN, 5TH DISTRICT OF TENNESSEE

"Sam and Stephen believe in the basic goodness and generosity of us all. Unlike many books that want us all to do more and be more (when we all already feel maxed out), *New Day Revolution* simply asks us to become the people we already want to become—and offers some simple and direct ideas on how to do it."

ANDERSON WILLIAMS
DIRECTOR OF OASIS COMMUNITY IMPACT, A 2006 FINALIST FOR
THE PETER F. DRUCKER AWARD FOR NONPROFIT INNOVATION

"This is a great how-to book that offers practical advice on changing one's lifestyle and values for the good of others. It's fresh both in substance and style, in content and presentation. I recommend it heartily."

DANIEL VESTAL
EXECUTIVE COORDINATOR, COOPERATIVE BAPTIST FELLOWSHIP

"Be forewarned: This book will tweak the lens through which you view your place in the world. With Ben Franklin wit and Bono savvy, Sam Davidson and Stephen Moseley scatter their reader-friendly seeds of intelligence, wisdom, and challenge. Smart, bite-sized reads that convince your capacity to change the world one day at a time."

DR. JAMES BARNETTE
PROFESSOR, MINISTER, AND AUTHOR, SAMFORD UNIVERSITY

"Sam and Stephen have done a marvelous job at bringing radical stewardship into a simple and intentional lifestyle. You'll be able to make a difference before you get out of the shower! What a difference a day can make!"

BO PROSSER
COORDINATOR FOR CONGREGATIONAL LIFE, COOPERATIVE BAPTIST
FELLOWSHIP

"What is nice and unique about the first CoolPeopleCare book is that you can use it like a guide book: no matter where you are, what you are doing, you can find an effortless way to make a difference but have a significant impact on the world on a daily basis. Everyone should always carry with him *New Day Revolution*! Bravo!"

CAROLINE BERNADI
CO-FOUNDER, FREEPLEDGE

HOW TO SAVE THE WORLD IN **24** HOURS

new day
revolution

XYZZY
PRESS

2007

SAM DAVIDSON and STEPHEN MOSELEY

FOUNDERS OF CoolPeopleCare

For information about permission to reproduce selections from this book, write to Permissions, Xyzzy Press, 9105 Concord Hunt Circle, Brentwood, TN 37027

Library of Congress Cataloging-in-Publication Data

Davidson, Sam, 1980-
New day revolution / by Sam Davidson and Stephen Moseley.
     p. cm.
Summary: "Gives helpful hints, practical tips, and step by step instructions on how to positively impact the local community and the world at-large with whatever time a person has"—Provided by publisher.
  ISBN 978-1-60148-004-0 (softcover)
  1. Social action—United States—Handbooks, manuals, etc. 2. Voluntarism—United States—Handbooks, manuals, etc. 3. Political participation—United States—Handbooks, manuals, etc. I. Moseley, Stephen. II. Title.
  HN65.D336 2007
  361.7—dc22

                                                                2007033342

A special thanks to Jeff Rossini for his input on the compost-bin recipe.

Design by Jay Smith-Juicebox Designs juiceboxdesigns.com

Printed in the United States of America
10 9 8 7 6 5 4 3 2 1

HOW TO SAVE THE WORLD IN **24** HOURS

new day
revolution

To our mothers,

Cynthia Moseley

and

Luanne Davidson

You were the first people who taught us how to care.

table of contents

introduction

HOW TO READ THIS BOOK

This is not your normal introduction. As you'll find out, we're not your normal authors, and this isn't your normal book. Most introductions don't get read. Most introductions are written after the rest of the book is complete. Therefore, most introductions are really (unread) conclusions. Hopefully, you're reading this, and we wrote this when we were only halfway done. Thus, like we said six sentences ago, this is not your normal introduction.

Introductions usually tell you where the book is going, what it was like to write it, and why you should feel good about the book you just bought.

Not this one. This introduction tells you how to read the book.

You may think you already know how to read a book. What more could there be than opening the cover, turning to the first page with words, and then moving your eyes from left to right? Your brain then handles the rest.

If it were that easy, then this would be the conclusion of the introduction.

But it's not.

This book is different. You don't have to read it like that. This book is yours to read however you like, depending upon your wants and needs at any particular moment. After all, you bought it (thank you). So feel free to read it however you want.

But here are some suggestions.

We've set up the book around the concept of a day, from the minute you wake up until it's time for bed. As you encounter each portion of your day that corresponds with a chapter in this book, you can move along the text, harvesting what you need. In this way, you can read the book straight through, starting at page one until you reach the back cover.

But you can also read this book by picking and choosing certain chapters. Because each chapter doesn't necessarily build on the one before or after it, each section stands alone. If you're going to the grocery store, skip to Chapter 7. If it's the weekend, and you're looking for fun and creative ways to save the world, turn to Chapter 10. Put the book in your purse or backpack, and take it with you to the coffee shop or to lunch.

You can also read within each chapter, gleaning tidbits of difference-making information by jumping around. Maybe you're someone who employs the thought-a-day format, in which case you might try doing one of our suggestions each day for the next several months.

If you're looking to save money as you save the world, look for the tips with a 🟢 by them. If you're looking to save fuel as you save the world, look for the tips with a 🔵 by them.

If you're in the mood for motivation, jump to the end of each chapter and read the Adding It All Up section. You'll feel inspired by the true tales of ordinary individuals who dared to save the world.

Saving the world is different for everyone. One person may feel compelled to replace his conventional toilet with one that composts human waste. Another may simply want to forego the environmentally unfriendly plastic bags at the supermarket line. One person might choose to sell all her possessions and donate the revenue to a local charity. Someone else might offer up an hour of her time to help a nonprofit organization balance its books.

However you want to change the world, this book is here to help you do it. With more than 100 practical tips on how you can save the world in less than 24 hours, *New Day Revolution* and CoolPeopleCare aim to be your best resource on how to make a difference.

We also aim to keep this book as current as possible, making it easier than ever for you to save the world. Throughout the book you'll see ✎ , indicating there's more information at NewDayRevolution.com. Online you'll find additional resources and other reputable Web sites, our recommendations for products we've tested and tried, and personal stories from other revolutionaries. We'll continue to update this site to aid you in your quest to make the world a better place. Information changes rapidly, new ideas happen, and we'll put it all at your fingertips.

The end (of the beginning).

up and at 'em

STARTING THE DAY RIGHT

The good news is, if you're awake, you're alive.
The bad news is, you have to get out of that
comfy bed, find something to wear, and at
least try to be someone who is pleasant to be
around. But before you have that first (and
desperately needed) cup of coffee, there are
a handful of things to be done that can make a difference.

The sunrise, the snooze button, and the shower can
illicit fear or excitement as a new day dawns. But how we
spend the first part of our days can have a lasting impact on
not just us, but on folks everywhere the sun shines.

Only 60 percent of us work a traditional 9-to-5 job,[1]
and that number is quickly dwindling as our economy
becomes more digitized and less traditional. We can now
work from home in our pajamas and conduct business over
the phone and the Web as if we were wearing an expensive
power suit behind a mahogany desk in a high-rise office
complex downtown. Some of us work nights, pull a swing
shift, or get called in on a moment's notice. As time passes,
fewer and fewer of us will wake with the rooster and work
until dusk.

In other words, when we get up is changing. One
person's 6 a.m. is another's 3:30 p.m.

But no matter when we get up, there comes a time when
we all open our eyes and hop, crawl, or zombie ourselves
out of the sack. We may stumble into the shower, the
kitchen, or the study to face the first hour of our day.

If breakfast is the most important meal of the day,
as some suggest, then the first hour of our day must be
equally as important. How we begin our day sets the tone
for the other 23 hours. At some point in time, we've all
had something happen early in the day that managed to
wreck the rest of it, leaving us begging for bedtime so that

things could improve by the time we wake up the next day.

When embarking on a revolution, the first small steps set us on a course of making a difference that will get easier as the hours tick by until we get to start the whole thing over again.

Annie Dillard wrote, "How we spend our days is how we spend our lives."[2] If that's the case, then how we spend our mornings may very well be how we spend our days. Getting things off on the right foot, starting the day off right, and waking up on the right side of the bed are crucial if we're going to get this revolution off the ground.

wake up earlier

If you have trouble finding time for yourself (or finding time to make a difference), then set your alarm clock to wake you up a few minutes earlier. (Warning: hitting the snooze button will, in fact, negate the effects of this experiment.) We all need our beauty sleep, but you may not even miss those extra minutes, especially once your body adjusts to the change. A few minutes here and there may not seem like much, but over the course of a year, you could get as many as **50 extra hours**[3] to use to change the world.

the first five minutes

Now that you've got some extra time, how will you use it? We believe that a revolution can happen in as little as five minutes a day. Take your first five minutes of the day and use it for you. Breathe in. Breathe out. Feel alive. Listen to your heartbeat. Feel the fan's delicate breeze against your skin. Be present. Listen to the sound of your lungs fill with air and feel that air move over those tiny little hairs in your nostrils.

Sure, it's gross, but stay with it. No matter what happens today, this time was your time, and you used it to be you.

navigation by touch

If it's still dark when you get up, see if you can make your way out of your bedroom without turning on any lights (which automatically results in that emergency squinting reflex usually employed when you leave a matinee movie on a sunny day). You know your way down the hall (including that spot where your dog sleeps and that other spot where your son left his shoes), so there's no need to flip every switch you pass. Why use electricity when you don't need to? Keep the lights off, and keep coal in the ground.

⑤ shower quicker

Who doesn't love the stream of warm droplets hitting their back each morning? But enjoying such a simple pleasure can get us in hot water (literally). Instead of your normal allotment of shower time today, try to shave one minute off of your time in there. By shortening your bathing ritual by as little as 60 seconds, **you'll save about five gallons of water.**[4] Sure, you'll miss that extra time where you're lost in thought while your super-duper massaging showerhead does its thing, but the environment will thank you. If you do this every day this year, **you'll save more than 1,825 gallons of water and $11 in utility costs.**[5]

toothbrush revolution

You may not think about it outside of the (ideally) three times a day you use it, but your toothbrush can be a vital instrument in changing the world. We all know that the water shouldn't be running while we're shining our pearly whites, but how else can this small thing save the world? Here are some suggestions:

> Instead of tossing it in the trash when you're done, make a nifty bracelet.
> Because you're supposed to replace your toothbrush every three months, think about investing in one that reduces waste, like those with replaceable heads.
> We like it when you think recycled, so try a (new) toothbrush made from recycled materials.

how do you rinse?

Some things tell us a lot about a person: what kind of music they like, whom they admire, and how they rinse when they brush their teeth. If you bend down and drink straight from the faucet (or if you're a tad more civilized and use your hand as a cup), make sure you turn off the water in between swishes. Or, if you use a cup, avoid the paper variety that is good only for a few times before you toss it. Instead, utilize a real glass or cup that you can put in the dishwasher every so often.

organic toothpaste

You may have heard the buzz about organic foods and, believe it or not, it's made its way to the bathroom as well (but not like that). Organic toothpaste is available, and it's good for both your teeth and the planet. Not only have these dental pastes not harmed the environment or been tested on animals, but they also can be less abrasive while whitening

your chompers after all that coffee and tea you enjoy. Visit
your local drugstore to see what's in stock near you.

NDR 101: WHAT IS ORGANIC?

Organic is a term typically applied to food. Usually this means that the food (if a fruit or vegetable) is grown without using pesticides, synthetic fertilizers, or genetic mutations. If the food comes from an animal, then it means that the animal wasn't given growth hormones or antibiotics. Basically organic food is grown in a way that is best for the environment, animals, and people. So when this term is applied to something like toothpaste or T-shirts, it means that the ingredients are treated in a similar fashion. Crops that go into the final product didn't have tons of pesticides or herbicides dumped on them, and the products themselves weren't unethically tested on animals. In addition, a lot of organic items are made locally, so you'll be supporting nearby growers and producers. All in all, these foods and basic needs have a much lower environmental impact. These products are usually a bit more expensive, but you can feel good about buying organic. And since more than **$30 billion worth of organic products are sold each year in the United States,**[6] this is more than a fad—it's a movement.

the makeup of makeup

In a similar vein, makeup can also be very harmful to lots of innocent creatures. So put your best face forward by buying products that treat animals fairly. We all want to look good, but feeling good is more important. Make sure that your lipsticks, deodorants, shampoos, soaps, blushes, and lotions are produced ethically. Your small decision to buy socially conscious brands is better for everyone.

wear something

For some of us, what to wear is the hardest decision we'll face in a day. Does our belt match our shoes? And does no white after Labor Day include socks? Who decides what's "hot"? As you get dressed today, throw on a bracelet, shirt, or pin that means something. Even though the risk of over-saturation is imminent, those rubber bracelets actually do make people stop and ask questions. Make a statement of both fashion and awareness today.

newsworthy

If the morning paper is part of your morning routine, take a risk and see what happens when you read about the world through a different lens. Harness the diversity of the Internet and read your news from a variety of sources. Get your local fix in print, and then venture online for a national and international check on what happened yesterday and why.

+ + + adding it all up

Most of the time, authors don't tell you why they chose their title. Maybe they lost a bar bet, maybe their editor has a lot of control, maybe it was written in the sand that time they went to Hilton Head, or maybe it's really obvious.

But since we're transparent kind of guys, we'll let you in on our title-picking process.

As we've been growing CoolPeopleCare, we've had a lot of promotional ideas. Some might call them gimmicks. We call them really-cool-ideas-that-most-people-are-scared-to-do-but-we're-new-at-this-and-will-try-anything-once.

We've thought about giving away go-carts, making a movie, getting Chip (our clever and cute mascot) tattooed on our bulging biceps, and even planning weddings. As you can see, some ideas don't exactly rise to the top.

But others do. And you're holding two of them.

As we began to write a slew of "5 Minutes of Caring" pieces in preparation for CoolPeopleCare. org's launch, Sam thought, "Wow. These would be great in book form." We thought that such an event would be years down the road, but as is often the case, things don't happen exactly according to our neat little plans.

Likewise, in the fall of 2006, we were thinking of a way to celebrate the new year. Some folks drop a ball in Times Square, some kiss each other at midnight, and others just sleep through Dick Clark's countdown. (Has it really changed at all over the last 35 years?)

We had heard of those things called New Year's Resolutions

that well-intentioned people make every January. In fact, we'd made some ourselves over the years. Sam had every hope of playing Major League Baseball, and Stephen really wanted that seven-figure recording contract but, as we've said, things don't always go according to plan.

So as we sat in our "office"—really, our favorite coffee shop—we wondered if there was a way to celebrate the new year without the broken resolutions that plague all of us. Could we highlight the things folks were doing to save the world, not just every year but every *day*?

Instead of a New Year's Resolution, what if we made New *Day's* Resolutions?

Let's face it—New Year's Resolutions are hard to keep. We don't know anyone who's kept one for 365 days. In fact, if you have, please contact us. Certainly some sort of award is in order.

We all know that our best-laid plans of January 1 all too often become our easiest failures less than a week later.

What if, instead of trying to do something for an entire year, we just tried to do something for one day?

When we look at it like that, the grandiose goal becomes manageable, which means we just might be able to pull it off.

What if, instead of saying, "I'm going to lose weight this year," we said, "Today I will eat a salad for lunch." And what if we did it? And then we tried it again the next day and the one after that? Then, before we knew it, we'd strung together a month of healthy lunches?

Then, our resolution became a *revolution* (and thus, the title).

What if, instead of saying, "I'm going to get organized this year," we said, "Today I will clean out that drawer in the kitchen that holds everything I'm looking for at any given moment?"

"I'm going to budget this year," becomes "Today I will spend no more than $25."

"I'm going to go green this year," becomes "Today I will recycle all of the paper I use."

"I'm going to help people this year," becomes "Today I will give $5 to a worthy cause."

We do those small things, keep our New Day's Resolution, and before we know it, we've got a revolution on our hands.

Some people took up the challenge:

> Dan, from Indianapolis, turns off the water while lathering up in the shower to save water.

> Katie, from California, wants to accept herself as she is, and not how others think she should be.

> Jane, from Nashville, wants to drink eight glasses of water a day.

> Azurae, from Seattle, wants to do one thing everyday for someone else.

> Suzanne, from Birmingham, wants to tell one person each day about the reality of poverty in America.

> Lynnette, from Fort Worth, wants to eat one meal a day that was locally produced.

That's the potential power of one day. You can do one good thing today that makes a difference. Add that to a long string of days, and you'll have a week, month, year, or decade of saving the world.

Today, wake up, and make a promise to yourself. Attempt to do something great and small. Try something new. Dare yourself to be spectacular. Change the world. Take that first step.

stop and go

MAKING PROGRESS IN TRAFFIC

The morning commute. Its utterance strikes fear and dread in millions of us. Maybe we don't like where we're going. Maybe we hate sitting in traffic. Maybe we can't stand the thought of spending time in the car away from things we would rather be doing, like changing the world.

Not so fast (pun intended).

The average American spends 100 hours each year just getting to their 40-hour-a week gig.[1] That's a year's worth of vacation time spent in traffic! Certainly we can reclaim this time and use it in a positive manner if there's so much of it.

Our method of travel may vary (car, subway, bus, covered wagon, bobsled), but we all have to get where we're going. And sometimes, how we get there is just as important as where we're headed.

There have been advances in how we work, which enables some of us to avoid the hassles of traffic jams and fender benders. We may work from home, telecommute, vary our hours, or even not work at all. But the fact remains that we'll still face travel time in some form if we want to leave our house.

No matter how far or long we do drive, our transport machines all have combustion engines that require what seems like the bane of our society's existence these days: gas. We all know that the less gas we use, the more money we save, which is why several of this chapter's tips will help you save gas, which is better for your bank account. And, **with almost 300 million cars on the roads of North America,**[2] every little bit of gas saved is better for the planet.

Even though we may think of this hour (or more) of our day as "wasted," the reality is that we can use our drive time to save the world.

In our lifelong quest to save you time, money, and your sanity, we've thought of some ways that you can re-examine your time in the rat race to benefit others and our planet. We don't see this time as a means to an end, but as a chance to rethink the ways we drive, ride, and get to where we have to be.

○ the pressure's on

Before you climb into your minivan or sedan, check to make sure your tires are properly inflated. By keeping your wheels filled with the proper amount of air, you'll make sure you're getting the most out of every gallon of that all-too expensive gas. By making your fuel last longer, you'll buy less and will therefore save money. Having the right tire pressure means you'll drive farther in return for the CO_2 you put out.

buckle up (duh!)

We shouldn't even have to remind you about this one: when you get in, buckle your seatbelt. You've probably heard it a million times, but lots of folks still ignore this practical safety tip that saves lives. Studies have shown that **63 percent of people killed in accidents weren't wearing seatbelts,**[3] and a simple click could have prolonged their lives on this planet. If you've got passengers, make sure they buckle up before you shift into drive.

don't go it alone

While some of us use public transportation like buses, subways, or trains, **75 percent of us still drive solo**[4] to get to work. The strain on the environment is growing, so why not buddy up? Check the bus schedule to see if you can easily get where you're going. Many local governments have rideshare information to promote driving less. Shoot out an e-mail, and see if a coworker lives near you.

○ ac or windows?

If you're not sure when the AC in your auto is most efficient, here's the rule of thumb:

> When driving in traffic, roll down your car windows instead of using the air conditioning; otherwise, you'll burn extra fuel.

> Keep your windows up when traveling on the highway. At higher speeds, your open windows add drag and **reduce gas mileage by up to 10 percent.**[5]

Using the right window protocol will save you money and conserve fuel.

○ no lead feet

We're all in a hurry because none of us thinks we have enough time. But making sure you obey the speed limit could save:

> Your environment (cars operate more efficiently and conserve fuel when driven at proper speeds).

> Your money (you could get pulled over and have to pay a fine and maybe increased insurance costs).

> Your life **(nearly 33 percent of all traffic deaths are speed-related).**[6]

We all want to go fast, but think twice before your foot

hits the pedal. Taking an extra minute to get where you're going will make a big impact.

what's that lever for?

For some of us, the least-used part of our car is the blinker (if you haven't found it yet, it's near the steering wheel). You can change that by employing its signaling features whenever you want to turn or change lanes. Make sure you don't pull the trigger too soon, and always flip it off once you turn. You may know where you're going, but the people behind you sure don't.

drive and learn

Anyone can listen to the same trendy radio tunes driving back and forth to the city each day. Why not drive and do something else at the same time (besides eating, applying makeup, or getting dressed)? While in the car, turn your radio dial to a program that will teach you something (besides the words to the latest bubblegum pop song). Spend your commute time today listening to a news program, an educational expose, or even a book on tape. Be careful—you may actually learn something.

after you

Even though you took Driver's Ed., you're still not sure whose turn it is at those pesky four-way stops, blinking red lights, or tricky roundabouts. Take the high road, and motion your fellow travelers to go ahead of you. You'll be sure to not waste time with a fender bender, and someone's day might be made a little brighter by your generosity.

end road rage

We've all been tempted to honk, scream, and give the finger. And although we may not admit it, we've all given in to such primitive urges. Today, if you are bumper to bumper, resist the temptation to call names. Instead of getting mad, get patient. Learn to say the alphabet backwards, count your teeth with your tongue, or memorize an inspirational quote. It will make for a happier trip through the asphalt jungle.

○ go roof rack-less

You may not tote around a roof rack much these days, but if you do need one when you hit the beach or the slopes for that family vacation, make sure you take it off your car when you get back home. Though it seems like an inconspicuous piece of car gear, the roof rack adds unnecessary drag and extra weight to your car. By removing this burly piece of equipment, **you could improve your fuel economy by nearly 10 percent.**[7]

trick your plate

You rarely think about your license plate except when it's time for renewal or when you leave your lights on at a concert. When it's time to renew, check the appropriate box, and get a plate supporting a cause you care about. It costs a little more to brandish an organization's name or logo on your back bumper, but this money is channeled toward your cause. You'll also be making a statement about what's important to you.

end potholes

No one likes it when they're cruising along, about to take a sip of their morning beverage of choice, and then a pothole appears out of nowhere, disrupting what was shaping up to be a decent morning. It's time to take action and fix our streets. The next time you pass a pothole (or drive right into one), contact your state's Department of Transportation, and report the gaping hole.

terrapass

For the price of a few CDs, you can buy a TerraPass and work to offset the CO_2 emissions your car pumps out every day. Short of buying a hybrid, this is the best and cheapest way to do your part to help fund clean energy from sources like wind farms or methane capture facilities. TerraPass calculates how much CO_2 your car puts off and offers a comparable package used to offset your personal auto's pollution by investing that amount in renewable energy sources. Plus you get a swanky decal for your car.

NDR 101: WHAT IS A HYBRID?

You've heard the buzz about hybrid cars, and you think they also look kind of cool. But how exactly do these things work? And are they worth it? By definition, a hybrid uses more than one source of energy. Most hybrid cars use a combination of gas and battery power to get from point A to point B. A hybrid's technology lets it know when to use which. For example, some models rely on the battery at very low speeds (like when backing out) or when stopped (like at a traffic light). This way, the car saves gas to use for acceleration, when the engine needs to move faster. In other words, a hybrid saves gas by using less fuel and by using that fuel only when it's needed most. When the engine is firing on fuel, it charges your battery, so there's no need to "plug in" your car. And, here's a secret: a hybrid may be more affordable than you think.

+ + + adding it all up

Joanna is 24 and lives in the very hot city of Tucson, Arizona. She is working her first job out of college and is passionate about caring for the environment and making cities more sustainable. She has student loans, an apartment, a cat, and a boyfriend. She goes shopping for groceries, picks up her dry-cleaning, takes out the trash, and cooks dinner. She does the things you do every single day.

She also drives to work five days a week. Her commute isn't awful. It's not two hours and 75 miles each way. It's what we'd call an average commute of 30 minutes or less.

But one day last year, she decided she wouldn't use her car for *an entire day*.

We're not talking about just carpooling or riding the bus to her job. We're talking about before, to, from, and after work—24 hours without a car.

It wasn't easy. She lives in a sprawling city. And even though she loves to bike, the trip to work was too far, so she had to call and search online for the local bus schedule. As is often the case with public transportation, the bus didn't come to her door and drop her off at the main entrance of her office. She had to walk nearly a mile roundtrip for the privilege of sitting next to strangers.

It also took some planning. Without a car, she couldn't do the things that we often take for granted. Think about it: without a car, you can't run and grab a soft drink at a nearby drugstore. You can't pick up some fast food you heard advertised on the radio just a few seconds ago. Trips to the bank or post office become inconvenient at best and impossible at worst. Not using your car for a day is a serious decision.

But the bus ride itself was beneficial. She didn't have to concentrate on other drivers or on speeding up and slowing down, so she was able to reflect and focus on her day. And she even noticed the beauty of the world around her—flowers, trees, buildings, people, and animals.

Joanna was able to make a positive impact on the environment, and the environment made a positive impact on her.

Even though it didn't soon become a daily habit, her

mission to take her car off of the road for a day meant something. Every car is different, but **the average car emits nearly 125 grams of CO_2 per mile.**[8] So this means that by not driving at all that day, Joanna saved seven pounds of carbon dioxide from polluting the atmosphere.

If she teamed up with a friend to carpool (and thereby drove half as much each year), she would save enough emissions equal to powering not just her apartment for an entire year, but the entire complex.

Joanna's ambition and courage to do one thing for one day shows the opportunity that lies within every hour for all of us to do good.

CHAPTER 3

taking care
of business

USING THE 9-TO-5 TO
MAKE A DIFFERENCE

Most all of us have to work (or have had to work), and unless we're one of the lucky few born into a life of idle luxury, we have to go somewhere and do something in order to be given money. With this money, we then buy things that we need, like food and shelter, and  things that we want, like video games and throw pillows.

Sure, there are alternatives to working, such as casino heists and winning lottery tickets, but for the majority of us, those things aren't exactly contingency plans. So we go for the guarantee that a steady job provides, and shuffle in and out of our offices in order to get home and finally do what we've been dreaming about all day: eating reheated spaghetti in front of the TV.

We spend almost a third of our adult life working,[1] so we really should try to find ways to enjoy it. A lot of us have found our dream job. Some of us have created it. Some of us do what needs to be done as we dream about our dream job and make the sacrifices needed to get us where we want to go. And some of us are just putting in our time until we get our gold watch, our pension, and some much-deserved time off.

Even though a bunch of us really do want to save the world, we may not exactly be up for living in a commune or wandering the earth as social prophets.

But we can still have a worthwhile impact while doing something of worth.

Even if you don't work on an assembly line, chances are good that there are parts of your job that are equally repetitive. Each day you boot up your computer, check the mail, hang around the water cooler, refill the stapler, or print something out. You sit in meetings, get put on hold, and help customers. You count money, restock shelves, or drop things off.

Let's face it: your job's not exactly like the ones those CSI folks have, but it's important that it gets done nonetheless.

So while we can't make your task of changing the printer's ink cartridge as awesome as what Jack Bauer does, we can show how correctly changing that printer cartridge can save the world.

how are you?

As you make the daily rounds, you probably ask "How are you?" as often as you get solicited yourself. Today, actually listen to the answer. Spending valuable time listening to someone's feelings will work wonders for a sense of community, and everyone can always use a listening ear. Instead of complaining to the folks in IT, see how they're doing. Instead of avoiding your boss, ask how the weekend was.

tell a coworker

At work today, tell a buddy about your church (or synagogue or mosque), your charity, or other favorite change agent. A quick mention of an organization you believe in will plant seeds of inquiry into the mind of another. Just drop a name or two at the water cooler or coffee pot, and leverage an existing friendship to get others involved in the work that needs to be done to transform the world.

NDR 101: WHAT IS A NONPROFIT?

Lots of folks we meet say they want to work for a nonprofit. But what exactly is such an altruistic entity of commerce? A nonprofit can come in a variety of forms, with the goal of impacting a lot of different situations. Some nonprofits are related to politics; others are religiously centered; and others serve as philanthropic arms of larger, for-profit corporations. Each of these promises that it will not make a profit, at least not in the sense that a business does, in which profits are paid out to the owners (shareholders, proprietors, investors, etc.). Instead, a nonprofit uses the money it gets (via donations or charging for services) and uses that money to affect change. Most nonprofits are called 501(c)(3) organizations. This means that when you write them a check, you can deduct this contribution on your personal income tax statement at the end of the year. When most of us think "nonprofit," this is the kind of organization that comes to mind. A lot of the day-to-day operations in nonprofits and for-profit businesses are similar—garbage needs to be emptied, payroll needs to be processed, and the copier still needs toner—but, depending upon how you're wired, you may enjoy working for a different "bottom line," as it were.

⑤ computer naps

Check the energy settings of the computer you're using. Most machines have the ability to put the monitor or hard drive to sleep when not in use (for PCs, right click on the desktop, and click on screen saver). If you're not surfing the Web for hours at a time, set your monitor to rest after five minutes of inactivity. When you're ready to leave work for the day, turn off your PC or Mac. **Doing so will use 80 percent less electricity and cut CO2 emissions by more than 500 pounds each year.** [2]

use the back

No matter what you do or where you work, chances are good that you'll need to print something. If you're just putting something on paper to proofread or peruse before sending that final copy down the line, use the backs of some previously used paper. Even though **Americans recycle nearly half of all paper used,** [3] lots of paper that is recycled is only half-used. So make a separate stack of clean-backed paper, and feed it into your printer next time you need to print off a rough draft or some notes.

$ printer cartridges

Each year, **nearly 300 million empty printer and toner cartridges are dumped into landfills.** [4] Nearly all of these could have been refilled and reused, saving your company money and saving the environment from more trash. Some office supply stores will refill the cartridges, so find out who your company's supplier is, and see if they're on board. Otherwise, you can buy the refilling kits online, and do your part to make your printer environmentally friendly.

flex some corporate muscle

Although we wish everything was recyclable, some things just have to be thrown out. After you're done with that project today, take the trash and make it as small as you can before tossing it. By compacting your disposable items, you'll save space in landfills. This is also a good thing to do with your cardboard boxes and aluminum cans as you recycle them. Make them small so that more can be toted to the recycling plant for processing. Try to throw away the bare minimum and, when you do, compact it to save valuable room in your garbage bags.

civility in the office

Pick one person, and say something nice to them today. Everyone can see a fake compliment coming from a mile away, so choose something unique, and be sincere. Replace "Your socks match," with "I enjoy the way you look at things from a different angle." Get rid of "You don't smell that bad today," and use "Your creativity is inspiring." Remember: the sincerity of your tone will convey just as much as the words you use.

digital donations

You can keep your desktop computers, phones, laptops, keyboards, printers, and other items with power cords out of landfills by finding a charity near you that can't afford the gizmos that are now commonplace. Your company gets a write-off, and a nonprofit receives some expensive and badly needed gear.

workplace giving

With a quick trip to your human resources office, you can get the ball rolling on donating some of your pay to a great cause. Organizations like United Way make it possible for you to allocate some of your pay to community organizations (some businesses will even match your donations). If your workplace doesn't have this option, tell your boss that it's badly needed. Or take the initiative with some coworkers to leverage the true meaning of teamwork. Have a food drive, put together a 5k team, or raise awareness about a social need.

+ + + adding it all up

We've got to eat to live, and we've got to work to eat. By default, then, we all have to do something that begets a paycheck. Some of us call this odious task "work," and the rest of us enjoy this long part of our day and don't generally see it as a bummer.

There are lucky ones out there who love to make a difference and have figured out how to make a living (and a life) by making an impact. Here's a snapshot of a few of them.

> Deborah, from Nashville, Tennessee, was shocked at the scant amount of attention paid to international injustices. Whether it was the plight of refugees in Darfur or the apathy related to environmental protection, she knew that something had to be done to call attention to the things that need changing. Her passions and talents collided, and Happy Monkey was created. Offering women fashionable shirts with socially positive messages, Deborah donates half of her profits to organizations making a difference in the areas of the environment or human rights.

> Paul, from Boston, did some research and discovered that there were too many T-shirts made by sweatshop labor and printed on non-organic cotton. So when he came home from his 9-to-5, he began dreaming about a clothing line that would produce sweatshop-free, fair-trade, organic, recycled shirts with socially positive messages emblazoned on

the front. After getting his systems and materials in place, Paul started clothing the world with tops that make the world a better place. His creation is Off Your Back Shirts, a socially-conscious business that sells clothing people love.

> Linda, also from Nashville, couldn't sit still when she began to learn about the realities of women leaving prison. For many women who are incarcerated, getting out is just the first in a long series of steps toward a productive and positive adulthood. Many re-enter society with little knowledge of the basic skills needed to get a job, open a bank account, or rent an apartment. Linda, along with a group of other motivated women, saw this need and acted. A few years and countless grant applications later, Linda is executive director of The Next Door, a nonprofit organization that aims to decrease the large percentage of female ex-offenders who will re-enter prison.

Sure, people take the leap and venture off on their own, but is it for you? We meet people nearly every week who tell us that they hate their corporate job and that they would like to come home at the end of the day and feel like they made a difference. Many of these folks are thinking about leaving their for-profit gig and jumping headfirst into the nonprofit sector.

And we tell them, "Not so fast."

We think it's true that every job in every nonprofit is one that makes a positive impact. Whether you're recruiting volunteers to feed the homeless or balancing the books to make sure the domestic violence shelter can operate next month, each paid task is usually needed. But if you think that simply pulling

WORKPLACE
REFORM

down a paycheck with a tax-exempt employer printed on the upper left corner will be your panacea of social consciousness, finish reading this chapter before you draft your resignation letter.

At CoolPeopleCare, we believe that social change doesn't happen by one person or group snapping its philanthropic fingers. We've studied the things that need changing and know that they won't happen overnight. True reform will happen only when a concerted effort by everyone (individuals, corporations, politicians, nonprofits) happens each and every day. Only targeting one of the above groups for change will leave a gaping hole too big for a single group to cover.

We've worked in nonprofits of varying size and scope. We've consulted, organized, and planned. We've written grants and recruited volunteers. It's not a walk in the park, but it's not the kiss of death either. Like any job, you've got to be happy doing it. No matter how much you may want to make a difference, if you can't stand driving (or riding) into work each day due to the fear and loathing of your task list once you arrive, then it's not for you and you won't be as effective, even if you are helping the uninsured get medical care or the elderly get the services they need.

We've found that the people making the most positive difference in the world aren't necessarily those working at nonprofits. We've found that those who make an impact do so every chance they get, even while working at a for-profit business.

You may even make a bigger impact working for a sleazy, humongous, abusive corporation than you will as a nonprofit entrepreneur.

Here are some ways to take your job and shove it in the right direction:

> How does your company make a difference in the

community? Is there a philanthropy or corporate-giving committee? Is there a foundation? If so, see how you can have a say in how that money is doled out. If not, sell your higher ups on why corporate giving is important.

> Get others involved. Chances are, your job puts you in contact with many more folks than you'll get in front of or alongside in any other venue. Post information about an upcoming fundraiser in the internal newsletter, or share data about the needs in your local community through e-mail.

> Increase the bottom line. We don't mean this in the money-grubbing, greedy, oppressive sense. The belief in multiple "bottom lines" is increasing. At first, there was a responsibility to shareholders to return a profit to the owners of a business at any cost. Then, there was also a responsibility to the employees, the folks who did the work that made the money that was returned to the shareholders. These people needed to be happy and taken care of in order to do that effectively. And now, a third bottom line has emerged, dealing with social awareness. Businesses have an obligation to shareholders, employees, and the community. Our world needs business practices that do no harm to the environment and help make a difference locally. If the folks in your organization are not aware of this idea, bring it to their attention.

We can't guarantee your overwhelming happiness by doing any of the things we suggest in this chapter. But, if you desire to make a difference in any given situation, you can "employ" (get it?) some of these ideas to save the world (at least during eight hours of your day).

cool beans

TURNING YOUR DAILY COFFEE ADDICTION INTO A DAILY DIFFERENCE MAKER

Even if you don't like coffee, you've probably been to a coffee shop.
And even if you're not one of the **108 million Americans who drinks coffee,**[1] you can still use the social setting that is the coffee shop to save the world.

We're writing this while sitting in our favorite coffee shop (don't worry—we didn't write the morning commute chapter while driving). The fact that we deliberately chose to write here was based on a set of compounding and integrated factors. Sam keeps his e-mail and Internet browser windows open (thanks to the free Wi-Fi) to see if anyone wants to distract him. Stephen occasionally glances at the 24-hour news channel showing on a wall-mounted plasma display. There are usually some good indie tunes by Nashville artists playing overhead. We know the owner of this place. There are comfortable chairs and lots of natural light. If we stay until lunch, we can get a delicious sandwich. And oh yeah, they do make a good cup of coffee.

The reality that the coffee shop is now its own destination is an impressive phenomenon and usually has little to do with anything java-related. While similar shops in Europe have been around for a while, independent retailers have capitalized on the coolness of coffee becoming our national social drink. Each week we meet people for coffee, but we could just as easily meet over root beer, ice cream, or chicken nuggets.

Coffee is not the point of the meeting, or even of the shop. In fact, we still have friends who refuse to fork over a dollar for the house blend at any establishment for the simple reason that they can save money making their own at home. But they are in the vast minority when it comes to the rest of the U.S.; Sam's wife makes a weekly trip to the coffee shop—*and she doesn't even drink coffee*.

You can blame (or thank) companies like Starbucks for helping the coffee shop become the proverbial "third place." In today's world, we spend most of our time at home, work, and now, the coffee shop. It's replaced our churches, our ball fields, our rotary clubs, our front porches, and our public squares as a viable meeting place, after-dinner stop, concert venue, and discussion forum. And **with more than 25,000 coffeehouses in the U.S.,**[2] these places will become more and more important.

So too is the need for us to think carefully when we enter one. If you're the average person (who just so happens to want to save the world), small changes in how you use and enjoy this time will add up to make big differences. Whether you frequent a local establishment for their blend of beans, pop in to the national chain only occasionally, need a tall mocha to keep you going in the middle of the day, or religiously sip a cup at home every morning at 6 a.m., you can employ the following ideas each time you drink this "black gold."

go inside

More and more coffee spots are adding drive-thru lanes in an effort to add convenience. No matter how long that line looks, we ultimately think we can save time by staying in our car and ordering through a speaker. But when we let the engine idle for a while, our car begins to spew lots of carbon dioxide without us moving very much. Do yourself and the earth a favor: park the car, and go in. Those few steps to and from your vehicle may make you feel a little better about what you're ordering inside.

make a friend

If you always visit the same coffee shop, take a minute to learn the name of the person pouring that delicious cup of joe. By learning his or her name, you'll become a friendly face in their daily routine of serving up hot cups of caffeine. Learning people's names is something a lot of us overlook on a daily basis, but taking a moment to remember that there is a story behind each apron increases the notion of community. Just please don't use your newfound knowledge to shout across the coffeehouse that you need a refill.

drink fair trade

The number of coffee blends is nearly infinite, so you can easily have your pick of flavors. But no matter how strong you like the stuff, make sure you're drinking beans that are fair trade. Buying fairly traded coffee (and other products) ensures that the growers and farmers of your beans are being paid a fair market value for their hard work. **With 75 percent of the world's coffee supply coming from small-scale farms,**[3] your choice of bean at the grocery store or coffeehouse will ensure the livelihood of someone who played a vital, though unseen, role in the coffee process.

order organic

If you want to go a bit deeper in the coffee selection process, ask your grocer or barista if they offer any organic or shade-grown blends. Organically grown coffee beans are those that haven't had any chemicals dumped on them in the cultivation process. And coffee that is shade-grown means that forests weren't leveled in order to increase

NDR 101: WHAT IS FAIR TRADE?

The term "fair trade" has become a sexy buzzword of late. Companies label their foodstuffs as fair trade (after a strict audit process) to ensure that consumers feel better about what they're buying. And they should—fair-trade products mean that you've paid a fair price for that coffee, chocolate, or tea you're enjoying. Because many impoverished countries rely on commodities like coffee for their chief export, there can be an abundance of beans. Due to supply and demand, this can drive down the value of coffee beans so that farmers are being paid pennies on the pound for their beans. In contrast, fair-trade groups organize and set a floor price for their coffee. For example, a fair-trade farming group in Ethiopia may determine that their beans can be bought for no less than a dollar a pound. Such a premium price allows these farmers to better sustain their families and communities. However, it doesn't end with price. Fair trade also ensures that democratic pricing processes are established and that purchasers invest in the local communities from which they're buying coffee. The entire process is designed to help local farmers sustain their livelihoods while providing us with delicious cups of coffee. So, in the end, the extra dollar or two you pay per pound is more than worth it as it returns an investment that can't be measured strictly in numbers.

output. Thus, a fair-trade, organic, shade-grown coffee blend is the best you can buy as it encourages and promotes sustainable environmental practices.

reuse the stirrer

You only use it for four seconds and then toss it—what's up with that? The coffee stirrer is something you use without thinking when you add your sugars, saccharines, and non-dairy creamers. But we want to bring it to your attention. With **500 million cups of coffee sold each day in the U.S.,**[4] those skinny plastic straws and thin wood strips add up quickly. The next time you grab your java, take along an item you can reuse when you stir, like a metal spoon (or just stash your plastic stirrer for later).

sweeten with caution

If you're like the majority of us and enjoy something to break up the dark monotony of a regular cup, pay attention to what you're adding. If you're trying to stay healthy, pour in skim milk or soymilk instead of pure cream. In terms of the sweet stuff, we all should cut back on sugar, but many artificial sweeteners have been linked to health ailments. So if you want the best of every world, choose unrefined, organic, fair-trade sugar.

take back the sleeve

If you aren't able to tote along your own mug (or request a ceramic one when you dine in), you can still change some habits to help save the world. Most paper cups usually leave the barista's hand accompanied by an insulating cardboard sleeve. When you finish your cup of coffee today, ask your local establishment if they can reuse your sleeve (if you haven't mindlessly picked it apart). If, for sanitation or other reasons, they don't, keep it handy for your next trip out for java. Or make a statement by going all the way and purchasing your own permanent sleeve.

$ personalize the mug

More than 44 billion paper cups are used each year for hot drinks.[5] When you do the math of how many of those might be yours, your imperative to offset a few of those with a reusable mug becomes pretty clear. Whether you're stopping in as part of your daily routine or making a random pit stop on your way to somewhere else, bring your own mug to fill with coffee or tea. Most places are happy to top off your travel mug, and many offer a small discount because they're saving money on some of their costs.

tip well

When you've completed your coffee transaction, make sure to drop a few coins or bills in the tip jar staring up at you from the counter. Dreamers and students often inhabit the hectic space on the other side of that counter, so do your small part to help them get where they're going. A few coins may seem like a small amount, but by tossing them in someone else's direction, you really could do something good. Even if you use credit or debit to save the paper receipt, add a buck to the total. We promise you won't miss it.

+ + + adding it all up

Whether you visit your coffee shop once in a blue moon or you drink several cups a day, small changes in your behavior really begin to add up. If lots of us make the commitment to saving the world at the coffeehouse, a revolution begins to spin its enormous and powerful wheels.

If you use your own mug every day this year, you'll save a tree all by yourself.[6] If all 108 million American coffee drinkers do it, then we can no longer measure the difference in terms of trees. *We'll have to measure it in terms of forests.*

Your small acts and changes of coffee-related behavior do have a positive impact in our world. Your effort toward reducing the waste related to ordering and drinking coffee or tea will save space in landfills, keep money in your pocket, preserve natural resources, enliven individuals and communities, and ultimately save worlds.

Revolutionizing this hour of your day may seem like a lonesome task in your corner of the coffeehouse, but you will not be saving the world in 24 hours alone.

An entire host of others with similar revolutionary ambitions join you in saving stirrers, returning sleeves, learning names, and leaving tips.

Among them are people like Molly, a barista at our favorite coffee spot. She's just a regular person who holds down a part-time job while going to school. Instead of shuffling in and out of this coffeehouse 20 hours a week for $7 an hour, she sought to use her job as a launching pad for change.

Molly asked the owner of this local beanery if she could help begin a recycling program. In less than a day, Molly had set up three large, labeled boxes in front of the pick-up counter. One box is for those glass bottles of soda they sell to folks not in the mood for coffee. Another is for paper that people generate while using the space as a temporary office. And one is for all things canned.

We asked the owner about this. She said, "This is something Molly wanted to do. She felt strongly about it. She also encouraged me to use our wine glasses for customers who just order water, instead of using plastic cups. I thought it was a great idea. Not only is there less trash, but it's one less thing I have to buy each month, saving me money." Molly is working for a paycheck like many of us, but also acting on her convictions in the workplace and saving the world in the process.

Then there's Jack, from Austin, Texas. Jack enjoys coffee and found out that he was spending a lot of money on his coffee habit every month. Quickly moving across the spectrum from casual drinker to delicately palated connoisseur, he decided he wanted to roast his own beans at home, saving him money.

Then he thought that if his beans were good enough, he could sell them to other people, and maybe even some restaurants. And he might make a little money in the process. So Jack bought some beans (no, not for a beanstalk), a bigger roaster that he housed in his garage, and started selling by the pound.

But he didn't just want to make a bunch of money while peddling fair-trade coffee. He wanted to set up a Paul Newman-like operation, channeling his profits to worthy charities. And so Jack roasts and ships beans, hoping that someday he can fuel his own passion into a way for people to pursue theirs. By eventually siphoning a portion of his profits from his hobby-turned-business, Jack will soon be able to help promote the work of other revolutionaries. If you want to try Jack's work, he has developed a coffee just for us, New Day Blend. You may purchase it at NewDayRevolution.com.

And you can join this coffee revolution as well. If you love the beautiful black and brown beans and a coffeehouse is as much a part of your day as your workplace and home, then do the things we recommend every day. If you only visit one at your leisure or on the weekends to catch up with a friend, do what you can during that time. And even if you don't ever darken the doors of one, share the word with your friends who do, or encourage the Mollys and Jacks of the world to change their worlds with passion.

The revolution will not come in giant buckets and mammoth barrels; it will come one coffee cup at a time. Preferably a reusable one.

surf's up

LOGGING IN AND
HELPING OUT

Seventy percent of Americans use the Internet! Believe it or not, that's more than double the amount that used it at the turn of the millennium and **triple the amount that used it just 10 years ago.**[2]

As you know, technology travels fast. Most of us have jobs that require the use of the Internet at least for e-mail, if not also for research, networking, selling, or communication. **The average person spends 48 percent of their free time online.**[3] In most places around the world, **the average person spends more time online than watching television.**[4]

The Internet has become as much of a place to make a difference as your local community center or your neighborhood streets. And with the rise of social networking sites and social cause applications, the Web is a place you go to, exist in, and interact with others. If the coffee shop is the proverbial "third place" as we mentioned in the previous chapter, then the Internet has to be a close fourth.

Online, you can make friends, just like you were at a local watering hole or a neighborhood gathering place. You can buy stuff, like you were at the mall or the local car dealership. And you can solicit the opinions of anonymous millions of other people, like you were at...well, like you were somewhere that was never possible until now.

But because it is possible now, we found it prudent to show you ways to surf the 'Net in order to make a difference. Your online presence is now as vital as your physical one, which means that your time spent there can make as much of a difference as the time you spend volunteering in your local community.

We don't think that the Web is a viable alternative to

making real, in-person friends—it's merely a complement. So log on and keyboard up as we offer some ways to make a difference in a digital world.

sign a petition

At any given moment, there are hundreds of petitions online that need signing. Most petitions are used to show elected officials what the people want. We recommend using Amnesty International to find a great cause and as an easy way to get your message to the people who need to hear it.

change your signature

Some people use their e-mail signature line to relay contact information, others use it to be funny, and some folks aren't even sure exactly what it is. Why not use the last line of your e-mails to draw attention to something positive? Include a quick link under your name to a socially aware organization you support. Even though it may seem like a small afterthought, a simple statistic or link at the bottom of your correspondence may catch someone's eye and make a big difference.

get a newsletter

Many nonprofits offer e-newsletters to keep interested individuals up to date on their issues and work. Today, sign up for one (or more) of these letters so you can stay in the loop regarding a specific cause. These online newsletters—which save paper—will make sure that you know about key events, fundraisers, wish lists, and success stories of your charity of choice.

cause auctions

Online shopping certainly offers the convenience of browsing in your pajamas and the environmental benefit of saving gas, but you can now do your best to make sure your purchases mean something. Ebay offers celebrity charity auctions, and you can also check to see if the people selling items you're watching are donating a portion of the proceeds toward a philanthropic cause. If you're the one doing the selling, earmark a portion of the price for a nonprofit near you.

NDR 101: WHAT IS SOCIAL NETWORKING?

If you don't know a 14-year-old to text this question to, maybe we can help. Although the term has been around for over 50 years, "social networking" today is used to describe Web sites that link people and their online profiles together in a network of "friends." The term quickly rose to household status when a site called MySpace launched in competition with another one called Friendster as a means by which bands could make new fans online. It quickly evolved to meet a much larger market and to date has posted more than 100 million personal profiles. MySpace profile pages truly (and crudely) do map relationships from one to another, allowing individuals to send their music, pictures, and incoherent ramblings virally down every avenue of the ever-growing social map. There are now many other sites out there to help you make friends and influence people.

just click it

In order to prove that you can get involved without getting up, we point you to the Animal Rescue Site. With just a click or two of your mouse (thanks to generous site sponsors), your hand-eye coordination provides half a bowl of dog food to a needy pet. You can do likewise at similar sites:

> Give a book to a child at the Literacy Site.
> Give a free mammogram at the Breast Cancer Site.
> Feed people at the Hunger Site.
> Save the rainforest at the Rainforest Site.

more giving (without getting up)

Other sites allow you to give like none other:

> DonorsChoose lets you easily provide resources for public schools and students.
> Charity Click Donation donates money to charities through advertising.
> GoodSearch pays nonprofits just for your curiosity.
> FreePledge turns online shopping into online giving.

Change your surfing habits, and change the world.

be an expert

It's not as hard as you think to become an expert these days. You could spend lots of money and time getting some advanced degrees, but we've got an easier way. Just pick a topic you wish you knew more about. Now bone up on it for five minutes every day on different Web sites. Read thoroughly and, in a month or so, you'll know more than you thought possible.

+ + + adding it all up

No doubt you spend a lot of time on the Internet. Your time online may be spent shopping, finding old friends, seeing what happens when you Google your name, reading news, or making news. And perhaps that's both the beautiful and scary part of the Internet—we can do whatever we want with it.

So what would happen if we used part or all of our time online to make a difference? We can incorporate the behaviors and tips we mentioned in this chapter, but we can also take the all-important next step and do good things to benefit others. We can also use our free Internet time to help save the world.

This is exactly what Seth wanted to do. He learned that the vast majority of people didn't donate any money to charity (other than their church) and he thought that in a land of affluence and influence, such behavior was sad.

Seth Godin is full of good ideas. (If you don't believe us, you can read any of his eight best-selling books.) He likes good ideas because good ideas are the ones that ultimately make a difference. So if he were going to reverse a problem as big as the lack of charitable giving in America, he would surely need a great idea.

And then it came to him. He knew that people naturally like to talk about things that interest them. This is the reason a lot of folks set up blogs **(there are now over 60 million of them)**.[5] But many times, people forget they have them, get burned out, or just stop caring.

OVER
60
MILLION
BLOGS

Seth also knew that people like money. Especially money they could earn for doing something they like to do, and might already be doing in the first place.

He put these two together and came up with a concept called Squidoo. Sure, it's a funky, quirky name. But it's one heck of a great idea.

Anyone can set up a page on Squidoo, writing about whatever they want. This is called their lens—how they see the world and what they think about what they see. Their lens can be seen by other similarly minded folks, and a community of sorts can be developed. The best part is that each person who has a lens can earn money (through online advertising) simply for having a viewpoint.

But it gets better. A person can choose to donate their earned money to a charity. So by thinking and writing about something you enjoy, you can earn money for a nonprofit you support. Seth told us, "Just a little bit of a person's time can have a positive impact forever. Every time their page is viewed, forever, they'll be earning money for charity."

Seth took a big problem (the lack of people who give to charity) and built an easy and painless way for people to give a nickel or a dime to charity. Seth let us in on some of the success stories so far for Squidoo. "We've got thousands of people giving nearly half of what they're earning to a charitable cause," he said. "Because of everyone's efforts, we've built a school in Cambodia, funded research on juvenile diabetes, and saved ferrets in Ohio." Beautiful.

You don't have to be a savvy Web designer or a best-selling author. You can be you, thinking your thoughts, writing your words, telling your story, and raising your money. By simply logging in, you're helping out.

Visit Squidoo, set up your page, start writing, and begin to see the revolution get off the ground as you support great organizations with your time online.

chow time

EATING FOR THE BENEFIT OF EVERYONE ELSE

Lots of defining moments have happened over lunch. Some people met their mate. Some people made a new friend. Some people negotiated the contract that secured the big deal for their company. And some people traded their apple for someone else's fruit snacks.

We all know that eating is crucial for survival. The necessity that is lunch can easily become a ritual, a nuisance, an afterthought, or a dream. We can power our way through a quick bite while we run errands, or we can spend the better part of an hour tasting, chewing, swallowing, and savoring every delicious bite of our bologna-and-mayonnaise sandwich.

Whether we're five or 95, we (in the U.S. are lucky enough to) eat lunch. Or at least we should. Sometimes we skip it in order to get something done, but when we do, we regret it come mid-afternoon. Other times, we order that extra cheeseburger, which we also soon regret.

Lunch can come in a lunchbox (thus the name), in a sack from a fast-food joint, or on a tray from a waiter. The method of delivery differs, as does what gets delivered. But we can all use our mealtimes to save the world.

Maybe your lunch hour is a reprieve from your monotonous work routine. Maybe it's not an hour but more like a half or quarter hour. Maybe you never eat alone. Maybe you put the "power" in the phrase "power lunch." Whatever the details, lunch is part of your vocabulary, and part of your day.

Americans spend more than $1.3 billion every day eating out.[1] There are **over 800,000 restaurants in the U.S.,**[2] and lots of them are crowded for lunch and dinner from sea to shining sea every single day. How we eat, then, is as important as what we eat.

Because the how and the what are equally important,

we bring you the following tips on ways to revolutionize your lunch hour in order to make a positive impact in your world. Every lunch is different, so tweak your culinary behaviors as you see fit in order to eat like never before.

ⓢ eat in

The benefits of not going out for lunch are quickly realized. By packing your lunch, you'll easily save money. You'll also save gas and environmental strain by not driving. Also, if you work at your desk, you'll be a multitasking champion, getting more done during lunch than most people get done all day. Or, it may allow you to leave work early, giving you more time to do something else that matters to you.

waste-free lunch

The average American child produces 67 pounds of trash a year just from their lunch.[3] And some of us grownups fare no better. Make a commitment today to eat a waste-free lunch. Here's how: fill your lunchbox (not a paper sack) with reusable containers (instead of plastic bags), stainless-steel utensils (in place of a plastic spoon or fork), a thermos (as opposed to a soft drink), and a cloth napkin (not a paper one). When you get home, simply wash, rinse, and repeat.

no plastic spoons

It's really convenient to drop one in your lunchbox, but the resources used to produce that plastic spoon have lasting environmental effects. Instead, bring along a metal version from home. It's much easier to wash one of these than it is to make one of the others.

⑤ eat a cold meal

Instead of cranking up the stove or the microwave for lunch, try eating a meal that requires nothing more than coordination and muscle power. Not only will it be a fun experience, but by eating a cold meal once a week, **you'll save about $1 and keep two pounds of coal in the ground.**[4] Do the math and, in a few months, you'll save a mountain or two.

go meatless

Try to eat a meatless lunch today. As tempting as a huge cheeseburger or meat-filled pizza is, opt instead for a salad or soy burger. These options save energy and animals. Who knows? You may even like the new fare, and it could lead to a lifestyle change.

get fresh

Frozen food requires 10 times more energy to produce than fresh food.[5] All of that preparing, freezing, packaging, and shipping really takes a toll on efficiency and the environment. For lunch today, do your part by eating one fresh meal. Resist the urge to nuke some prepackaged delight, and instead reach for whole fruits, organic veggies, or even some tasty treats from the deli.

eat it all

Only order what you can eat, and eat what you order. With **the average household throwing away more than 470 pounds of food each year,**[6] perfectly delicious food is wasted. Pack up your leftovers for a later meal (or as a

NDR 101: WHAT IS A FARMERS' MARKET?

Even though the big-box retailers may save us money and offer incredible convenience, hauling all those goods across the country takes its toll on our local communities. It's also easy to get lost in the sea of thousands of customers on any given day inside one of these stores, so any sort of personalization or recognition you hoped to gain while you shopped for tonight's dinner is nearly impossible. But checking out a Farmers' Market might change all this. These markets allow the growers themselves to bring their fruits and veggies right to you. By cutting out the middle man (or woman), there are many benefits: you get to know the people growing what you're eating, a lot of this food is produced organically and is therefore healthier, you keep your money in the local community, and someone's hard work pays off. You may pay a bit more, but you can feel better about it. Also be on the look out for growing and farming co-ops (known as Community Supported Agriculture or CSAs) near you. Many of these allow you to buy in to that season's crops and pick them up on a weekly basis, adding healthier and fresher items to your table.

gift for someone else). We also suggest eating at restaurants that serve reasonable portions.

⑤ skip the soda

We know the immense necessity of your Diet Coke fix, so we've got a challenge: pass on the canned soda and give your drink money to someone or something that needs it. You'll save calories and some aluminum from needing to be recycled, and your loose change can be given to someone who asks. Saving your drink costs for the entire week makes a larger donation to a worthy cause. Drink water for lunch, and pass on the savings.

decline the extras

If you're not bringing your lunch from home today, turn down the extras available when ordering out. Remind the person taking your order that you won't need plastic utensils or paper napkins with your order (or that long-lasting plastic bag they're wrapped in). Reduce waste by nixing the stuff you really don't need.

go topless

Even though water is obviously healthier, you inevitably will make stops at a fast-food joint or coffee shop to get your quick caffeine fix. Do your best to eliminate the waste from this experience and decline the top and straw they push on you.

waiter, waiter!

If you're sitting down, be sure to be nice to **one of the 2.2 million people who call themselves a waiter or waitress.**[7] Make an extra effort to treat your server with enormous gratitude and heartfelt respect. Learn their name, smile, say "please" and "thank you," tip well, and fill out a glowing comment card.

the lunch mixer

Today, when you grab your grub, ask someone to join you. Find someone you've never eaten with, someone you've never spoken to, or someone you know needs a friend. If you're feeling generous, treat them to lunch. When all of us sit and sup with a stranger, the world shrinks tenfold.

+ + + adding it all up

Brittney isn't some hardcore vegan hippie (not that hardcore vegan hippies are bad; she just isn't one).

She is a self-proclaimed pesco-vegetarian, but she doesn't have an elaborate vegetable and grain garden in her backyard. She doesn't inquire about the distance traveled from tree to mouth of each apple she eats.

She tries to eat healthy food. She has a food budget she tries to stay under each month. She goes to restaurants and grocery stores, just like we do.

She enjoys eating veggies and abstaining from meat for lots of reasons: it's better for her, it saves a little bit of money, and it's better for the earth.

Then she read a book.

Brittney picked up a copy of John Robbins' *Diet for a New America*, which called her attention to a few more things she could do to make her dietary impact even less.

Her pesco-vegetarianism is good enough in most people's eyes. **Fewer than 20 percent of us don't eat meat.**[8] The environmental impact of raising meat for consumption is huge, not to mention the terrible treatment of animals by most of the food industry. After reading this book, Brittney felt strongly that she needed to change her diet even more to reduce her impact on the plant and animal worlds.

She wasn't going to move to the forest and start eating tree bark and dirt.

She knew that she could simply order differently when eating out or shop differently at the grocery store and make a big difference.

For her, deciding to go vegan (instead of simply vegetarian) was an easy decision to make. But it wasn't about holding herself to some impossible standard. She did so because she didn't want to tacitly support the way chickens and cows are often treated. She did it because she didn't want to be fed at the hand of an industry that accounts for nearly half of all the water consumption in the United States.

By making a few changes in her food choices, she was reducing suffering, environmental abuse, and health risks. By eating differently, she was eating with a positive impact, saving the world three square meals at a time.

But she's not fanatic about it. Sometimes she eats cheese or orders fish at dinner. But she doesn't beat herself up about it. She just makes sure that the next time she eats, she does her best to reduce her negative impact.

You may not be ready to take the leap into vegetarianism or veganism, no matter what the benefits. And we don't expect you to toss out your freezer full of steak and hamburger patties or to stop ordering chicken nuggets "cold turkey." But what if you tried one vegetarian meal this week? Or one vegan appetizer? Or one local dessert? **If everyone in the U.S. ate one locally produced, organic, vegetarian meal each week, we'd save one million barrels of oil.**[9]

Tastes like revolution.

buying and selling

FLIPPING COMMERCE ON ITS HEAD

The mall is one of those places that some people love and everyone else loathes. If we think back far enough, a significant portion of our teenage years might have been spent at the mall for some reason or another. Maybe we were shopping for the latest styles, meeting friends to sit and talk  in the food court, or walking around in circles, hoping that our appearance at the mall would increase our cool factor by 10.

But, as we got older, perhaps we began to understand the mall and other errands truly for what they were: necessary evils. And even if we've limited our number of trips to the mall down to the weeks leading up to a birthday or holiday, the fact remains that we've still got to get in our car, drive to various stores, and exchange the money we've earned for the goods we want.

Since there's no escaping it, then we might as well embrace it. Most of us make at least two trips a week to the grocery store, and we'll stop at a retail or discount store another time as we get what we need to face the week.

We make lists, clip coupons, buy in bulk, and are willing to try almost anything new, all in an effort to save time and money. We fill our shopping carts and stand in line, waiting to open our wallets and purses to reach for the checkbook or credit cards.

It all makes us a little nauseated sometimes.

Can we redeem this seemingly unstoppable machine? Can we really revolutionize this system of free enterprise that has made America what it is ever since the first nail was sold to the first carpenter at Jamestown?

Most of us aren't able to eschew the economic system that is capitalism and take our families and set up shop on our own island, appointing ourselves Czar or Premier while we establish alternate systems of economic exchange. We badly want to throw off the shackles of the way the things are currently done, but at the end of the day, we still really want our Diet Coke and our kid still really needs those crayons. Maybe tomorrow will be a better day to overthrow the government.

But maybe we can keep our drinks and crayons and still shake things up. Maybe it's not that we're shopping but rather *how* we're shopping. Retail giants rake in billions a day before most of us go to lunch. It's time to save the world while we shop. Doing what we can when we arrive, move through the aisles, check out, and head for home will make a difference.

◐ plan and combine

Whether you hate errands or like to use them as an excuse to get out of the house, you can be more efficient if you save your trips and make them all at once. By going to all of your local merchants in the same outing and carefully planning your route, you'll save gas, the earth, and some cash. We're not saying you have to buy everything from the one-stop, big-box retailers but, the more you can get in one spot, the better.

take an extra step

When you go shopping, park as far away as you can. While the extra .0001 mile of driving saved to the front of the lot will be minimal in terms of fuel conservation, you will get a few extra steps in, which has some health benefits. Also, you free up a closer space for someone who may be a bit sore in the toes or needs to be even closer while they parade their babies in from the car.

⟳ pull forward

Even though it may seem small, pulling forward in parking spaces saves gas. While you won't always have an empty spot in front of you, take advantage of it when you can. This way, you won't burn gas when backing out of your spot, just to shift gears to go where you needed to go in the first place.

the shopping cart

Today, when you go to the store, move a shopping cart from the middle of a parking lot to the front of the store on your way in. Or just find a random one, and return it. Better yet, if you can time it right, take it from someone who just loaded their goods into their car. You may make a friend and experience retail karma—hopefully you won't come out to find an annoying ding in your door.

take the bag back

500 billion plastic grocery bags are consumed worldwide each year.[1] These bags are often used once and then take eons to disappear. The next time you go shopping, take your old bags with you. Buy a bag holder for your pantry, and grab a few sacks to reuse (or recycle) at the checkout line. Better yet, ditch the plastic bag altogether, and take your long-lasting canvas (or other material) bags every time you go to the store.

buy two

During your next trip to the grocery store, buy an extra of each non-perishable food item on your list. (Ask your cashier to bag those items separately.) On your way home, swing by a soup kitchen or food pantry that needs the items. Now you won't be tempted to give away the expired food in your pantry during the next canned food drive. This also works well with pet food (and other supplies) for animal shelters.

shop socially

What you buy says a lot about what you believe. Add these alternatives to your list the next time you visit the grocery store:

> Soy Milk—it's full of protein and is better for the environment and animals.
> Fair-Trade Chocolate—knowing that people were paid a fair wage makes this delight taste even sweeter.
> Environmentally Safe Cleaners—many stores carry non-toxic and chlorine-free cleaners, making not only the earth safer but also your home.
> Recycled Goods—certain situations may require paper products, so some stores offer recycled paper towels, napkins, and other items.

NDR 101: WHAT ARE CARBON OFFSETS?

Within the green movement, there's been a lot of talk about carbon offsets and carbon credits. Meaning the same thing, these phrases center around the idea that you can offset— or get credit for—the ways you emit carbon in your daily activities. For example, if you put out 15 tons of carbon a year by the way you travel, use electricity, or eat, you can buy an equal amount of renewable energy. So if you drive a lot, emitting lots of harmful CO_2, you can purchase carbon credits that make it as if you were running your car with renewable energy. Some people think it's a great idea, and others think it's an easy (but expensive) way to feel good about your energy consumption. And, like anything else, there are people trying to make a quick buck on a carbon scam. Do your research if you want to head down this road.

made to last

Before you make a purchase, think:

> Is what I'm buying durable, and will it last for a long time?

> Can it be repaired if it breaks, instead of being thrown out?

By making sure you really need what you buy, and by making sure that what you buy is long-lasting, you'll save money and space in landfills.

use less packaging

They're sexy, and they make us want to buy the products, but all of those wrappers, cans, and boxes typically become useless when emptied. Make it your goal today to buy items with less packaging.

> Buy 2-liter bottles instead of cans.

> Get the big coffee tin rather than the smaller ones you buy more often.

> Say no to those items that look over-packaged.

> Decide to eat fresh fruits and veggies.

And then, think creatively about ways to reuse those empty containers.

+ + + adding it all up

We all have to buy stuff. If we want to eat, stay warm, smell good, and have places to sit when company comes over, then a trip to the supermarket or store is inevitable.

Meet Jody. She knew she had to shop. She considers herself a part of society, and thus accepts all of the social responsibilities that come along with that. She makes sure she's presentable when she goes to work, and she keeps a nice house.

But she also knew about the immeasurable suffering of those in other countries where shopping would be a dream. We complain about long lines, clamor over a price break, and squeal when there's a "buy one, get one free" sale. But such a world is completely foreign to many people in the world.

And Jody knew this. And Jody decided to act.

She decided she would go as long as she could without buying anything new. Well, not *anything*. She kept things like food, deodorant, soap, and milk—items needed for physical and social survival—on her list. But she crossed off CDs, new clothes, home décor, and fuzzy dice. If she needed something, she'd see if she could borrow it, trade for it, or do without it.

She was obviously saving money—after all, when you're not buying a new watch, a magazine, or a Frisbee, you can pocket some cash. But, oddly enough, Jody didn't have any more money. Surely she wasn't stocking shampoo for the apocalypse, was she?

As it turns out, Jody was using her savings to provide clean water for people in Africa. And she was sponsoring children each month living in poverty in other countries. And she was donating money to local charities that mean something to her.

Jody doesn't make big bucks at her job, but she's as philanthropic as they come. She saw a need and felt as though she had to do something.

By cutting back on her shopping, Jody was able to meet the needs of others.

A small, everyday behavior was changed for the benefit of people she'd never meet. Now that's an economic revolution.

Do your part to refrain from buying what you don't need. The extra money you'll have is great, but it's better if you can direct it toward someone who needs it.

CHAPTER 8

home ec(ology)

SAVING MONEY BY SAVING ENERGY

The biggest energy guzzler out there isn't our minivan or our SUV, rumbling down the street as we shuffle the youngsters to soccer practice or sleepovers. For most of us, our home is the largest consumer of fossil fuels we own. **Although Americans make up only five percent of the world's population, we use 26 percent of its energy.**[1]

Whether you're in a tiny apartment or a large house on a cul-de-sac, your abode is using coal, oil, or natural gas to power the things you enjoy as part of your daily routine. Your television, microwave, and hair dryer need the juice of the grid to do their thing. And when you plug these things in, flip them on, and enjoy their unique powers, you're using energy, no matter how long it takes to dry your hair.

Furthermore, unless you live on a wind farm or have installed solar panels, your energy use has a direct impact on your monthly bills. **The average American family spends $1,900 a year on energy.**[2] Each and every one of us would love to save some of that for more enjoyable things like ice cream, amusement parks, or charitable donations.

The formula is pretty simple actually. The more energy you use, the more you pay. And the less energy you use, the less you pay. (Who said math was hard?)

Likewise, the more energy you use, the more natural resources are stripped out of the ground, the more pollution is put into the air, and the more you leave an irreversible footprint upon this earth of ours.

The more energy you can save, the more money and planet you can save. Win, win.

But sometimes we get stuck in a routine and like the

way we do things. Sometimes, it's easier to leave a light on overnight, run a washer full of water but low on clothes, or use water like it's going out of style (water, by the way, will never go out of style).

To break you out of those harmful household habits, we've got these quick and easy tips that you probably didn't learn in home-economics class. These ideas can be incorporated easily by the entire family to make sure that the little ones grow up in a home that is earth friendly.

⑤ audit yourself

In less time than it takes to clean the baseboards, you can go online and give your place of residence an energy audit. After answering some detailed questions, see what changes you can make to save money and the environment. Some may be quick fixes and others may be long-term investments, but you're guaranteed to see a difference.

⑤ unplug that charger

You know that cell-phone charger you keep plugged in downstairs? It could be costing you $30 a year in electricity. Lots of our appliances sap electricity just by being plugged in. This phenomenon is called "phantom loading," and **the average household uses 450 pounds of coal a year**[3] just to keep DVD players and computers plugged in.

⑤ change the bulb

How many Americans does it take to change one standard light bulb in their homes? Hopefully every single one. **If every American household changed their five most-**

used light fixtures from regular light bulbs to energy-saving incandescent bulbs, the energy savings would be the equivalent of taking eight million cars off the road, saving $6 billion in energy costs for the nation![4]

NDR 101: WHAT ARE COMPACT FLORESCENT BULBS?

The buzz about compact florescent (CFL) light bulbs is bright. CFLs are almost immediately recognized, even by people who have never bought one—they've got that trendy, curly-Q look. But, other than the look, these bulbs are super cool. The beauty is that they use a lot less energy than a regular, incandescent bulb. The older bulbs that we're all familiar with use heat to create light, which is why they're famous for burning fingers after being on for only a few minutes. While these bulbs are cheap and burn bright, all of the heat used to produce the light escapes as energy. When you turn on a light that uses an incandescent bulb, you're paying for heat you'll never use. A CFL bulb is different. CFLs produce light without creating all of the heat, saving you money on your energy bill. While CFLs cost a bit more, they last far longer, saving you money in the end. CFLs do contain scant, non-dangerous traces of mercury, so make sure to clean up quickly if a lamp gets knocked over.

how to cook

Here's how to make dinner while saving energy and time:
> If you need to heat something, zap it in the microwave, saving time and energy.
> If you use the stovetop, don't use a pan bigger than you actually need.
> Don't use a burner that is bigger than your pot or pan.
> If you're boiling water, put a lid on it. This will help the water heat faster.

⑤ refrigerator etiquette

For maximum efficiency, keep your refrigerator at 38 degrees (no cooler) and your freezer at five degrees. Don't leave the door open as you stare blankly at those leftovers, wondering how long they've been in there. While you're at it, check your door seals and replace worn insulation if some of that cold air is escaping. If you've got an ancient icebox, upgrade from (and properly recycle) that older model.

⑤ fill 'em up

When it's time to clean those dirty dishes or wash those dirty shirts, make sure your dishwasher or washing machine is full. By waiting to use these appliances when they are full of plates or pants, you will maximize your use of water, detergent, and the energy used to heat the water. For your washing machine, always make sure you're using the appropriate water level, and use cold water as often as possible.

$ dry your clothes outside

Use your dryer less. If you don't have a clothesline out back, string one up in your living room, or invest in a drying rack. By not using your electric or gas-powered dryer for a month, **you can save up to $5 and keep about 10 pounds of coal in the ground.**[5]

$ check your bottom

Take a minute and look very carefully at the bottoms of your exterior doors. Unbeknownst to you, valuable energy could be escaping through your doorframe. If you can feel a draft, or if you can put a sheet of paper in the door, close the door, and remove the paper without it tearing, then you need to improve the seal. The quickest fix is to install a door bottom or a door sweep. Any hardware store will have what you need to correct the air leak.

$ flip your fan

If you've got a ceiling fan, use it to regulate the temperature in your home. In the colder months, you want the fan to be pulling air up from the floor, which will circulate the hot air near the ceiling to the rest of the room. In the summer, you want it pushing air down, keeping things cool. In most cases, this means the fan will be rotating counterclockwise for the summer and clockwise for the winter. If your fan is spinning backwards, just flip its switch to reverse the direction.

$ your air filter

By replacing the filter in your heating and cooling system, you'll increase its efficiency, ultimately saving you money while preserving the natural resources your home consumes. You should be doing this at least every three months (or more often, depending upon your HVAC system), so if you can't remember when you last swapped it out, now might be a good time. Plus, doing this means you should be able to breathe just a little bit easier. Write the install date on the filter so you know how long it's been in there.

⑤ look for leaks

When you get home from work, before turning on any faucets or flushing any toilets, take a quick glance at your water meter (it could take 30 minutes for water to cycle through your plumbing system, so do this when no one's been at home). If the dial is moving, you've got a leak somewhere that needs fixing. See if any faucets are dripping, and listen for leaks in toilets or pipes. If you spot the leak, learn plumbing basics quickly, or call your local plumber. While you're outside checking the meter, make sure your garden hoses aren't leaking any water.

⑤ use your windows

No matter how many windows you have, you can utilize the handy natural sunlight they let in. Look around at some of the places where you spend the most time at home that requires light. Where is your desk? What about that comfy chair you curl up in to read a good book? And where do you look at the newspaper or the mail? Consider relocating these locales near a window so you don't have to turn on a lamp during the day.

⑤ south-facing windows

If you live in the United States, your south-facing windows receive the most sunlight and heat throughout the day (north windows receive the least; the east and west ones get hit hard, but only briefly). By opening the blinds or curtains during the daytime, you allow in natural heat and light. But, to stay cool(er) in the summer, keep them covered so you won't need the air conditioner humming incessantly.

buy green power

Fortunately, more and more utility companies are getting some of their power from renewable sources (like wind and sun). But this technology is expensive. To offset that cost, you can buy units of green power and do your part to make sure that the energy you use is renewable. Check your latest power bill for details.

+ + + adding it all up

Our energy use as Americans is overwhelming, to say the least. But numbers and math can be pretty impersonal. What does it actually look and feel like when you dare to engage the home ec(ology) revolution?

Meet Jeff and Heather. These two crazy kids got the wild notion that maybe they could make a few small changes at their home to keep some coal in the ground and save some money in the process.

Their motivation wasn't entirely monetary, however. Jeff had seen firsthand the terrible effects that mining has on the environment. He had talked extensively with people living in places like West Virginia or the Carolinas who've watched as entire mountains nearby have been destroyed in order to provide us with the ability to warm up leftovers or turn on our porch lights.

Jeff began to explore the various methods of alternative energy. He was amazed at the power of our wind and sun to provide the juice our homes need to keep us warm (or cool).

But he and Heather weren't exactly in a position to erect a windmill outside of their basement apartment. They knew they couldn't throw up a solar panel or install a geothermal system. Such an investment was beyond their means at the time; however, they could do something. They could do their small but important part to reduce the amount of coal and oil they used each day to watch television and run their ceiling fan.

They started by using energy less. They made sure a light was off if they didn't need it. They turned off the AC when they went to work and only ran their dishwasher and washing machine when full. They opened their windows to use the magical, cooling powers of a breeze.

Then, they revolutionized the way they used energy when they had to use it. They upgraded their old, incandescent bulbs to compact florescent ones. They traded in their old, energy-guzzling refrigerator and bought a certified energy-saving one.

Instantly they preserved some natural resources. On their very next electric bill, they saw a decrease in the amount of kilowatt hours they consumed, which meant they were using less coal to power their home. And, of course, using fewer kilowatt hours to power their machines and appliances meant they were spending less money. They had cut their energy use down to 500 kilowatt hours and were saving $25 to $50 a month.

But they didn't go splurging their newfound savings on Caribbean vacations or big-screen televisions. Wanting to further their impact, they used their savings to buy blocks of green power. This way, their utility provider could employ more uses of alternative energies. Indirectly then, the power they were using was coming from renewable sources. They used their savings to buy 750 kilowatt hours worth of green power, so Jeff and Heather were as close to being off the grid as they could be, short of living in a windmill.

Their changes were small, but important.

The things they did were easy, but crucial. But the results they got were huge. They saved some cash as well as entire mountains and hillsides from destruction.

The small steps mentioned in this chapter will help you save money, but more importantly, they'll help you save the world. You can get more ideas and even watch Jeff and Heather in action in their film about energy use, *Kilowatt Ours*.

CHAPTER 9

cleaning up and cleaning out

REMOVE CLUTTER AND MAKE THE WORLD A BETTER PLACE

Sadly, doing all the things necessary to make your domicile environmentally friendly (and money saving) won't also clean out the junk in the closet or garage. All of us have wished at some point that a magic genie, gnome, or flying monkey would appear and instantly whip our house into shape.

But unless you live in a cartoon or children's book, it ain't happening.

Most of us want to get rid of the stuff that we don't use. We want a nice, tidy place to call home. We sometimes spend our weekend or even weeks on end straightening up and sweeping out. And it always seems like just when we clear one square foot of carpet space in that spare bedroom, someone in the family brings in a new (old) item to clutter it up all over again.

But if you're really serious about running a tight ship, we've got some ideas to make sure your abode is junk and clutter free, and to help you cut down on **your yearly trash production of more than 1,500 pounds.**[1]

We have no doubt (and also no scientific proof) that lots of the needs of clothing and food in the world could be met by what's in all of our pantries and closets. We've all got shirts and pants we haven't worn in more than a year. Useful items are going unused by taking up space in our homes and apartments.

All while many around us go without.

We could buy a box of trash bags and go to town (and then to the dump) with all of the stuff we want to get rid of. But because there are so many in need, it's better to get creative and see how we can make a difference letting others reuse what we already have.

Following some of these ideas will allow other folks

to put your goods to valuable use. And overall, more and more items will be kept out of landfills.

Win, win, win.

stop the junk

We all love getting mail but, after a while, the stack of credit cards applications and other junk mail gets less and less exciting. The **average American receives about 500 pieces of junk mail every year, weighing nearly 30 pounds**[2]—the equivalent of about one and a half trees. But there's hope: you may enroll to have your name taken off of those lists.

⑤ unconventional reuses

What if you could keep stuff out of both the trashcan and recycling bin? Here are three common items and ideas for reusing each of them:

> Cardboard rolls from toilet paper or paper towels can be used to store plastic bags from the supermarket.
> Used dryer sheets in your pocket can repel mosquitoes during spring and summer months.
> Old coffee grounds keep away garden pests.

give a coat

Many of us have too many coats while there are others who don't even have one. Make a commitment to give one jacket to a local shelter or clothes closet. You may only wear it a few times each year but, for someone else, it's daily protection from the elements.

all those hangers

If you're doing some spring cleaning, grab your extra hangers, and get rid of them properly. First, see if your local dry cleaner will take them. This saves them from having to buy new ones. If they won't, just visit the hanger recycling center near you. If all else fails, have a campfire cookout with a hundred or so close friends.

give vision

Whether you switched to contacts, your prescription no longer works, or you went all the way and had laser surgery, there are a number of organizations that can use your old spectacles. Try to find a group near you that collects the frames and provides free eyewear to those in need. With **over one billion people around the world in need of glasses,**[3] your pair can really make a difference.

don't flush medicine

When cleaning out the medicine cabinet, make sure you properly dispose of your old and expired medications. While it's easy to toss them in the trash, these pills can easily find their way into the wrong hands. Don't flush the pills either. The old capsules can make their way into our streams and waterways, harming wildlife. Instead, collect all out-of-date bottles, and take them to your local pharmacist who will know how to properly dispose of them.

recycle your batteries

Batteries can unlock, compute, record, play, and call. But they can also pollute lakes, expose water to acid, and much more. Keep an extra recycling bin (alongside your aluminums and plastics bins) for household batteries. Drop them off at your nearby recycling center, and help save the earth.

collect your grease

When preparing your dinner, pay attention to the fats, oils, and grease you generate. These are the by-products from meat, cooking oil, shortening, and butter. When poured down the sink, grease tends to collect and build up as it moves through your plumbing system. This can cause blockages in your city's sewer line, leading to nasty backups and raw-sewage pollution. Collect your culinary by-products in a sturdy, leak-proof container, and take them to your local recycling center.

how to paint

Before you rush off to the hardware store to purchase a few gallons of paint, keep in mind these environmentally friendly tips:

> Cut down on harmful vapors by making sure cans are covered at all times.
> Use non-toxic, latex, low-VOC (volatile organic compound), biocide-free paint.
> Reuse brushes, rollers, pans, and drop cloths to reduce waste.
> Properly dispose of old or unused paint.

With **Americans spending $17 billion on paint each year,**[4] a few small changes really add up.

all those leaves

Every year, residential yard waste takes up space in landfills and contributes to water pollution by plugging up city sewers and storm drains. Instead of leaving your fall foliage to rot on the ground or dumping your leaves in with the trash, mulch it for composting. If your city has a leaf collection program—which you can find on your local government Web site—rake your leaves into biodegradable bags, and place them on the street for pickup.

NDR 101: WHAT IS BIODEGRADABLE?

Technically, the word "biodegradable" is an adjective used to describe something that is capable of decaying through the action of living organisms. Nature biodegrades everything it makes back into the earth. Hence, a truly biodegradable product came from nature. But over the years, "biodegradable" has been misapplied to products like plastic because there aren't any official guidelines in regards to proper labeling. A plastic bottle will never biodegrade. Ever. But just because a product came from nature (e.g. a paper bag) doesn't mean that it will necessarily have an opportunity to return to its roots (no pun intended). A paper bag left loose, littering the land, will biodegrade in perhaps two to five months. But the same paper bag taking up landfill space won't because the conditions for biodegradation aren't optimal. Of course this isn't a license to litter—it's a cause for recycling. And if recycling isn't an option, it's a mandate for reuse.

police your pet

When you're out walking your dog, cat, ferret, or llama, make sure you pick up after them. Not only are their droppings a menace to the soles of your neighbor's shoes, they are also an environmental pollutant. Rainwater easily sends animal waste into our sewage system and, eventually, our rivers and lakes. Many families have at least one pet, so you can imagine the difference this would make to our noses and waterways if everyone did their part. You can even collect their waste in biodegradable bags.

+ + + adding it all up

The facts about our trash and the realities of recycling are nearly unbelievable:

> Americans throw away enough aluminum every three months to rebuild our entire commercial airline fleet.[5]

> Recycling a four-foot stack of newspapers saves a 40-foot tree.[6]

> Every glass bottle recycled saves enough energy to power a 100-watt light bulb for four hours.[7]

> In the United States, 63,000 garbage trucks are filled every single day.[8]

The benefits of recycling are clear. If you don't have a recycling program near you that takes care of household paper, glass, and plastics, write your elected officials, rally your neighbors, or stage a protest. The environmental and economic benefits of recycling should be obvious enough to everyone, and we should strive to incorporate recycling into the fabric of our daily society.

But what about those items that can't exactly be recycled—

at least not in the same way that plastic bottles or cardboard boxes can? What do we do with that old couch, or the toys our children outgrew, or that extra bedroom set now that we've moved into a smaller place? After all:

> **U.S. waste per capita has more than doubled in the past 40 years from 2.5 pounds per person per day to nearly five pounds a day.**[9]

> **Only two percent of all waste is municipal solid waste. The rest is industrial. Even if we could eliminate all of our household trash through recycling, reusing, and composting, 98 percent of all trash would still exist, just to make the stuff we use.**[10]

> **By reusing a sofa, you'll keep the 100-pound sofa out of a landfill, and you'll also keep as much as 20 times that in raw materials from being used.**[11]

Working full time for a nonprofit in Tucson, Arizona, Deron knew just how much useable stuff was being discarded. And he knew that a computer desk or loveseat couldn't necessarily be recycled. But it could be reused.

Deron's nonprofit's warehouse was filling up with perfectly good household items that had been donated or salvaged from dumpsters. Deron badly needed to find new homes for all of it. He thought that there were people out there who needed the things that other folks were throwing out, but he wasn't exactly sure how to connect the two.

In his quest to keep stuff out of landfills, Deron set up a community listserv, whereby anyone who needed to get rid of something that someone else could still use could let others around Tucson know that it was free for the taking. He sent out the first e-mail to a handful of folks, letting them know about the availability of furniture and other goods, and before he knew it, lots of people were interested.

In less than six weeks, his idea blew up. And in six months, there were more than 20,000 people on the listserv, listing and picking up each other's stuff. What was once someone's trash became someone else's treasure.

Almost immediately, what started as a grassroots campaign to keep stuff out of landfills became a way for anyone with an e-mail address to "freely recycle" the things they don't use anymore. And that's how Freecycle™ was born.

Now with more than 3.5 million participants in over 4,000 communities, people visit Freecycle™ in over 75 countries. All of this growth happened in just four years. All because one guy wanted to make sure that a filing cabinet a nonprofit could use wouldn't end up sitting in a landfill for all of eternity.

Deron shared with us what he feels makes Freecycle™ so popular. He hears from people everyday who realize the environmental, economic, ethical, and communal benefits of participating. For him and this community, it's really all about living a simpler life.

"People are finding that it's easier to give something away than it is to throw it away," he said. "And in the process, the notion of community is strengthened. One family meets another when they go pick up some old toys. They start a conversation, one thing leads to another, and a new friendship is created. We're really using the Internet to create a true sense of community."

It seems the revolution really can happen one dining

room table or box of stuffed animals at a time. Take a look around your home. What can you do without?

Begin giving away what you no longer need to individuals or nonprofits that could use it. It's better for the environment, and you may make a new friend in the process.

CHAPTER 10

weekend warrior

PUT A POSITIVE SPIN
ON YOUR FREE TIME

We've all heard TGIF. But it seems like it should be TGISa or TGISu. Why not—it's the weekend, after all! We've spent the previous five workdays dreaming about relaxing and having fun, so it's time to get started.

Weekends are always too short, and the best ones usually leave us quite tired come Monday morning. Regardless of how we spend the weekend, the point is exactly that—we can spend it however we want. We can go to the pool and grill out in the summer, shop, read a book, take a nap (or six), go for a jog, cook brunch, or take in a movie. We're off the clock, and it's time to have fun.

But just because we get to sleep in doesn't mean that the revolution is put on hold until the alarm clock strikes 6 a.m. on Monday morning. Time off from work doesn't mean time off from saving the world.

Most of us will use the weekend (or any of our free time, for that matter) to spend valuable, irreplaceable time with the people we love. Maybe this is why we look forward to the weekend the most. We want to see that band, go to that new restaurant, or take a one-of-a-kind vacation, but we want to do it *with* someone.

When we do something in community with others, the revolution spreads like wildfire. By saving the world with a friend, spouse, child, boyfriend, or aunt, we might be able to do more good than if we quit our job to try and save the world full time.

So, grab a friend (or six), and follow these free-time tips to have a blast and make a difference.

join the club

Museums and other organizations often rely on memberships

to offset some of the costs of their services. Membership has many benefits; depending upon the organization, dues are often tax-deductible, enrollment can be done online, and sometimes there are members-only activities. Nearly all of these places offer a family discount. Find a spot the kids enjoy, and have some free-time fun with your loved ones.

NDR 101: WHAT IS TAX-DEDUCTIBLE?

Giving is good. Unconditional giving is great. But it's also potentially beneficial to keep track of your financial giving, since the U.S. government wants to reward you for such thoughtfulness if you file taxes and itemize your deductions. Public charities, nonprofits, and foundations are the recipient of financial contributions, and due to their 501(c)(3) status you may write off your monetary contribution. But just because an organization is tax-exempt (meaning they themselves do not have to pay income tax), doesn't mean giving them money will necessarily be tax-deductible. If it matters to you, make sure to check a potential recipient's tax status first.

A few other items of note regarding charitable contributions:

> The value of volunteer time or services to a charitable organization is not tax deductible.

> Direct contributions to individuals are not tax deductible.

> The fair-market value of goods donated to a thrift store are tax deductible only if the thrift store is run by a charity.

We're not accountants or lawyers, so when in doubt, check with the IRS. When you can't understand their answer, find a good tax advisor.

⑤ check it out

At the library you can dive into their newspapers and magazines, freeing yourself from paper-wasting and costly subscriptions. Many libraries also have great family activities, so check out your local branch for some good family fun. And if your local library is within walking or biking distance, that gives you the chance to burn some calories as you borrow a book.

have a conversation

Talk to your family. See how everyone is doing, share a highlight from the day, and truly listen to what everyone has to say. You can also use an extra minute or two to send a family member or friend an e-mail or text message, just to let them know you're thinking of them.

movie choices

If you're looking for some weekend entertainment, why not take in a documentary or some other film that raises awareness? More and more movies with a purpose are hitting the silver screen. Whether you're staying in and renting, going out, or driving in, choose a movie that makes you smarter.

party for a cause

Whether the theme is birthday, Halloween, or luau, parties get lots of people together for a common goal: fun. Add a social cause on top of that and make a difference. At your next shindig, have each attendee bring a canned good or school supply with them. Collect all the items of your partygoers, and drop them off at a place that could really use them. Or take five minutes between party games to enlighten everyone about a topic you feel folks need to be aware of.

keep in touch

Scroll through your internal phone book, and find a person you haven't talked to in the last six months. Call them. Right now. Tell them thanks, that you love them, or that you miss them. Send them that weird picture you took, and make them laugh. Wish them well, and make a promise to call them more often. And then call them a month from now.

plant a row

Whether you enjoy tomatoes, carrots, or eggplants, you can use a row in your garden to produce tasty food that is good for you and others. With **more than 25 million people in the U.S. suffering from poor diets,**[1] you can take extra food to your local food bank in order to help out. Do your part by offering some soil for this valuable cause.

turn off the tv

Turn off the television and do what? Read. Talk to your children. Write a letter. Exercise. Call a friend. Rest. And the list goes on. **The average child spends 1,680 minutes each week watching TV.**[2] Choose one night a week to be TV-free, and see what newfound passions blossom.

travel size

If you take your own toiletries when you travel, those small bottles of shampoo and conditioner in hotels aren't of much use to you. Why not put them to good use by taking them and donating them to a place in need? Some organizations distribute the soaps to homeless individuals to freshen up. Others hand out the hygiene supplies to people staying overnight in hospitals with sick loved ones. If you don't travel much, swing by the store and grab a handful of the small deodorants or lotions, and drop them by somewhere that can use them.

+ + + adding it all up

Tamara seems like a regular mom (most of us know there's no such thing as a "regular" mom, but you know what we mean). She drives a minivan, carts her children where they need to go, and tries to teach them lessons and morals that will ensure they become the kind of people who want to save the world.

Before she had kids, Tamara did some stints as a substitute teacher. She was trying to do what she needed to do during the day (earn money) so she could do what she wanted to do at night (be a professional singer).

In between writing songs and practicing guitar, she went to different schools and filled in where needed. She didn't earn a ton of money, but she did enjoy being around children.

Soon she found a way to hone her singing skills while in the classroom. Once, while trying to keep the kids on their best behavior until the end of the day, she offered them a bribe. If they could make it the whole day without any major behavioral incidents, she'd sing with them for the last 15 minutes of class before they went home for the day.

And it worked. Why wouldn't it? Most kids we know would be happy to trade social studies for a sing-a-long.

Tamara began to incorporate character lessons during the singing time. She discovered that as she sang, she had a captive audience. If she could use their attention to teach them lessons that could prevent the misbehavior she was trying to stop by offering her singing as a trade-off, she just might be able to get the students to behave appropriately on days she wasn't there.

And it worked.

And Tamara had something.

Soon, in addition to writing songs, she began to write curriculum. She took the concept she pioneered and played it out for an entire year. In no time at all, she had 24 week-long lessons dealing with character education, all of which could be done in just 15 minutes per school day.

Tamara became the founder of Love in a Big World, a nonprofit that provides this curriculum to schools all over the country. With the help of great children's literature and willing teachers, students in elementary schools in several states began to learn the lessons of honesty, friendship, and hope that they weren't getting in their day-to-day science, math, and English lessons.

So Tamara is a mom who now leads a nonprofit that seeks to help families and schools develop positive character traits in children.

What can you do with your family today that will instill the values you hope to pass on for tomorrow? Often times, we think of inheritance in terms of money and property. But the best legacy any of us can leave is a positive influence. In as little as five minutes a day, we can instill lasting values of volunteerism, selflessness, and love in future generations.

That's how you turn five minutes into a lifetime.

happy holidays

CHRISTMAS IS NOT YOUR BIRTHDAY

Unless you're Isaac Newton, Jimmy Buffet, or Clara Barton, you already know that Christmas is not your birthday. Regardless of what month you were born, you also know that consumerism is rife during the holidays. Retail stores in the U.S. are filled with shoppers **who will collectively spend nearly half a trillion dollars.**[1] Advertising will lure you to buy things for others and to ask for things from loved ones.

We wonder what would happen if people began to rethink the time and energy spent during this time of eggnog, wrapping paper, and family.

If the average person spends nearly $1,000 each December,[2] what would happen if we decreased our budgets by just 10 percent and gave that difference to charity? We'd generate over $40 billion for nonprofits and worthy causes. That's change-the-world kind of money.

But it's not easy to break old habits, especially ones that involve swiping our credit cards and dishing out presents to people we love the most. Such a large movement begins with very small steps.

This chapter is full of ways to make Christmas (or Hannukah or Kwanzaa or Eid ul Adha or Yule) not your birthday. Incorporate just one of them into your holiday traditions this year, and make this holiday more about giving and less about shopping.

be thankful

Make time in between your usual traditions, such as turkey, football, and naps, to make a list of everything you're thankful for. Grab a pen and paper, sit down, and write a list. Set a timer, and see how quickly your list grows over the course of five minutes. When time's up, keep going. If people appear on your list, call or write and thank them.

turkey choices

Turkey has been the staple of many holiday dinners over the years, and your home is probably no different. This year, we recommend trying a free-range, pasture-raised turkey. These fowls have had access to the outdoors and the freedom to roam as far as possible without flying too high. If you're feeling daring, skip the meat altogether and give tofurkey a try. It's the same idea, but with tofu instead of meat.

buy nothing day

On the day after Thanksgiving, challenge yourself not to give in to the temptation to shop like mad. *Adbusters* spearheads a "Buy Nothing Christmas" campaign every year to help people realize that unbridled consumption isn't good for us and that continuing down this reckless path will further deplete precious recourses.

want differently

Eliminate one item on your annual wish list and put in its place something that benefits a charitable organization. Turn that trendy shirt into a yearly membership. Exchange that shiny gadget for a flat donation to a charity of your choice. Trade that new game for food for the hungry. Instead of asking for clothes to replace the ones that are perfectly fine, ask your parents to buy clothes for someone else. Instead of requesting the gadget that will be outdated by June, ask your spouse to send that money overseas.

Instead of it being all about you, make it about someone else.

dump your change

In 2006 holiday donations enabled the Salvation Army to assist 34 million people[3]—and that's just with what you had in your pockets while you were leaving the department store. Imagine how many people could be helped if you took all of your loose change to those nice folks in Santa hats ringing bells near those bright red kettles.

decorate wisely

When you pull that tangled ball of Christmas lights out of the attic, make sure you're doing what you can to conserve energy and natural resources:

> Regulate all of your holiday lights with timers.
> Use LED light strands instead of conventional sets. (Light-Emitting Diode bulbs last 10 times longer than CFLs—see Chapter 8—and are cool-running and bright-shining.)
> Store everything in recycled boxes.
> Reuse an artificial tree or make sure you purchase one from an environmentally friendly tree farm.
> Skip the Mylar plastic tinsel.

With a few simple steps, you can keep your house bright—and green—this winter.

cook twice

We challenge you to cook twice the amount you were planning for your holiday meal and take the extras to

NDR 101: WHAT IS RECYCLED PAPER?

Wrapping gifts helps us get into the spirit of the season, so make sure it's a spirit that keeps on giving. Seek out and use recycled gift wrap, and make sure to recycle the leftover paper scraps. Better yet, why not creatively reuse paper you've got lying around the house (old newspapers and magazines, packing paper, last year's gift wrap) to wrap your presents? Paper of all kinds can range between being made from virgin fibers to 100 percent post-consumer recycled. Paper from virgin fibers comes straight from newly cut trees (it takes two to three tons of trees to produce one ton of virgin-fiber copy paper). Those are trees that wouldn't have to be cut down if the demand for such paper was zero. Plenty of available paper is recycled, meaning it either came from paper scraps from the paper-mill floor, or it's "post-consumer," meaning it's been recycled from paper you once took to the recycling center. Recycled paper is just as affordable as non-recycled paper, and **it uses 44 percent less energy to create while reducing greenhouse emissions by 37 percent.** Check the label on every paper purchase you make, and give a gift wrapped in paper that can keep giving. And giving.

someone you know in need. Chances are, you'll toss out a lot of what you cook for yourself anyway, so be smart and see who needs some help nearby. Many families can't afford a decent holiday meal, so play Santa Claus (red suit optional) and offer up a delicious dinner. If time is of the essence, get a to-go meal at a local restaurant and play delivery guy or girl.

give twice

If you've never donated in someone's name or given livestock, this holiday season is the perfect time to start. As you give gifts with your specific tradition, find ones that donate a portion of the sticker price to a worthy cause. Begin family traditions that value sacrifice over consumption and giving over getting. You can spend the amount you planned to, but direct it toward things like protecting a child for a year, reuniting families, or feeding a village.

diversify your celebration

As jingle bells jingle and yule tides yule, take a few minutes to bone up on another winter holiday. If you celebrate Christmas, learn about Hanukkah (there's more to it than the candles). Or learn about Ron Karenga's role in starting Kwanzaa. Find out what Abraham has to do with Eid ul-Adha. Other things go on in the winter besides a jolly fat man coming down your chimney.

family time

Holidays are about family, whether you see them everyday or once a year. Use the opportunity of seasonal gatherings to enjoy your time with those who share your last name or blood type. Put on a smile and try to learn more about your loved ones. Listen to Grandma's stories. Laugh at your uncle's jokes. Reminisce with your weird cousin. Relate to your brothers and sisters. Help out your parents in the kitchen. Talk to that guy in the corner who shows up every year (but no one knows why). Be present and pleasant.

holiday recycling

Whenever it's time to pack up the decorations and relatives, make sure you do so in an environmentally healthy way. If you bought a real tree and you're not able to plant it in your yard, check to see if there is a Christmas tree recycling center near you. Before tossing out the packaging and boxes that hid your gifts until it was time to open them, look to see if there are places that can reuse these resources. Gather the rest up, and make sure as much as possible lands in recycling bins instead of garbage dumps.

+ + + adding it all up

It was Luanne's 49th Christmas. Certainly each of the preceding ones weren't exactly the same as the rest, but they weren't exactly memorably different either. There was always a Christmas tree, there were always presents and family, there was always a big dinner and, of course, Santa always made an appearance.

But when she decided to make Christmas not her birthday in 2006, she made a difference and some great memories. In the process, she rediscovered the true meaning of the holiday season.

By taking small steps to offset her spending and keep her desires in check, she gave to those in need, helped others, and changed her small part of the world.

If you ask Luanne, it all started with a Web post about spare change. It made her think about her glass jar, with coins she had collected on daily walks. This was money she was planning on saving for something significant, like a dinner at a nice restaurant or a new jacket. Suddenly the jar didn't represent savings but rather selfishness and greed. So she decided to go in search of the nearest red bucket with the accompanying bell-ringer. After emptying her change into the bucket, she promptly stopped by the recycle area to deposit her glass jar.

Coincidentally, that same day she read in the newspaper that a coffee shop was collecting coats. Having a daughter who had recently cleaned out her closet, Luanne decided that perhaps she could care once again. She paid a visit to the coffeehouse and dropped off the coats.

Her impact on this one winter day was pretty significant:

> A less cluttered counter from disposing of a jar of change, which became a donation that would help someone in need.

> A tidier closet from fewer coats, which went to folks who could really use them.

> A cleaner environment from a little less stuff.

As she thought about it, she realized that the personal impact she made was pale in comparison to what she actually received. Because she dared to care, she made somebody else's world a little better.

But she stopped to think: "Is this really what I would want for my birthday? Somebody's leftover coins and unwanted coats? Is this what I would give to those I love the most—stuff I really didn't want anyhow?" At that moment, Luanne decided to use this Christmas to do for others what she would do for her own family.

Luanne normally spends $100 on each of her five immediate family members. Her family had already decided to spend less this Christmas, limiting their individual spending to $25 per person. But she had originally been planning on spending $500 total. So she decided that she would spend the money, just on people she had never met.

Luanne went on a shopping spree of sorts and spread out the remainder of her allotted holiday spending at various local charities, providing much-needed donations for wonderful organizations that spend their time meeting the basic needs of others every single day.

Last Christmas, Luanne gave to more people than in her previous 48 Christmases combined. She made the commitment to make Christmas not her birthday, but others'.

the revolutionary in you

TELL YOUR STORY

Most books might try to tie everything together nicely with a succinct conclusion. Not us. Not here. Not this book.

That's because there is no conclusion to the revolution. Because this movement is one of our daily actions, behaviors, and habits, it goes on. Forever.

The good part is that we keep adding to it. We've all got a story of revolution to tell, and so this book ends with yours. Use this space to tell your story. Share the things you've done to make the world a better place. And then visit NewDayRevolution.com to share your story with others.

recipes for revolution

PROJECTS TO TAKE IT
TO THE NEXT LEVEL

If you've done everything so far in this book, then congratulations—you're a revolutionary. Now your duty is to tell others out there how they, too, can engage the New Day Revolution and change the world in 24 hours.

And if you're itching for more ways to make a difference, we offer you these one-time projects to help you continue to make the world a better place.

recipe for revolution #1

INSTALL NEW AERATORS ON YOUR FAUCETS

You're already taking the first step of conserving water by watching how often and how long the faucet runs. But how much water do you actually need to rinse off that toothbrush or wash your hands?

You can control the time the water stays on and—you might not know it—but you can also control how much water your faucet spits out by installing a new faucet aerator on your bathroom and kitchen sinks. (**Most sinks use three to four gallons of water per minute, though the government put in place regulations for any faucet made after 1994, mandating no more than 2.2 gallons per minute of flow.**[1])

Low-flow aerators add air to the water coming out of the sink, providing the same amount of water pressure, but using considerably less water.

> **INGREDIENTS:**
> > Aerators (one per sink)
> > Wrench
> **Approximate Cost:** $10
> **Time:** Less than 30 Minutes

STEPS:
1. **Hit the hardware store.** Aerators can be found in any hardware store's plumbing section. You can even choose how much water you'd like to allow per minute. We recommend getting the ones that allow 0.7 gallons per minute or less for maximum water savings. If you don't have an ordinary monkey wrench, pick up one of those as well.

2. **Find a sink.** If you can't find the sinks in your house, you may be in the wrong house.

3. **Unscrew what's currently there.** This should be very easy to do, no matter what type of faucet you have. It's like unscrewing the cap of a soda-pop bottle. From the back of the package:
> Remove old aerator with pliers, being careful not to grip too tightly.
> Check faucet for any washers that may be caught inside.
> Install new aerator by hand, turning clockwise.
> Turn on water. If leak occurs, tighten with pliers.

4. Repeat steps three and four for every sink in the house.

RESULTS:
> Water savings up to 25 percent per faucet.
> Peace of mind knowing that doing a little can save a lot.

recipe for revolution #2

UPGRADE TO A DIGITAL PROGRAMMABLE THERMOSTAT

A thermostat is on that list of stuff you don't think or worry about until it's not working—like the elevator, your remote control, or a long-term relationship. But if you're looking to take a big step in saving money and the environment, focusing on the thermostat is your best bet.

Depending upon when your house was built, you probably have a manual thermostat (in which a needle controls the temperature) that cannot be programmed while you're at work or away on a trip. Unless you can remember to flip the needle right or left or to switch the entire system off, your house stays comfortably cool most summer weekdays, even when it's only occupied by your pets and your furniture.

While this task may seem daunting and highly technical, do not fear: it's easy, even for the non-handymen and women out there. And, if you're still worried, your new thermostat will have its own set of directions, so you won't need to rely exclusively on these.

INGREDIENTS:
> Digital Programmable Thermostat
> Screwdriver
> Drill
> Hammer
Approximate Cost: Between $50 and $100
Time: About an hour

STEPS:
1. **Pick your thermostat.** Most hardware stores will have a wide selection of digital programmable thermostats, some with lots of bells and whistles. Find one in your price range you're comfortable operating and is appropriate for your lifestyle. Getting one with the Energy Star logo maximizes your energy savings.

2. **Switch off your furnace and air-conditioning breakers.** It is dangerous to remove your old thermostat and install a new one while your HVAC is still connected. Do not skip this step!

3. Uninstall your old thermostat, and label the wires.
You'll need to properly connect the correct wires to your new thermostat, so label the heating and cooling wires accurately.

4. Properly dispose of your old thermostat. Most needle-based thermostats contain small amounts of mercury, so make sure you properly get rid of the old model.

5. Drill mounting holes for your new thermostat.

6. Connect the proper wires to the digital thermostat.

7. Mount the thermostat on the wall into the newly drilled holes.

8. Put in new batteries.

9. Switch on the heating and cooling breakers.

10. Program your new thermostat for when you'll be at home and away, awake and asleep.

RESULTS:
> Reduced utility bill.
> Conservation of natural resources.
> Satisfaction of making a difference.

recipe for revolution #3
BUILD A COMPOST BIN

Composting is an environmentally beneficial way of recycling much of the waste we humans produce on a daily basis. Not only does it reduce the amount of waste we send to landfills, it also provides a wonderful garden additive of a plethora of healthy nutrients to the soil and plants.

Anybody can start a compost pile without spending a lot of money since the opportunities for composting range from do-it-yourself piles to commercially built, worm-assisted bins.

Compost is the end-product of a complex feeding pattern involving many different organisms such as worms, insects, bacteria, and fungi. The end product is a brown, earthy, nutrient-rich substance that is found in every forest, jungle, grassland, and garden on earth.

INGREDIENTS:
> Composting Bin
> Worms (optional)
> Organic Waste
> Shovel or Pitchfork
Approximate Cost: $25
Time: About an hour

STEPS:
1. **Find some space.** For the average household, 10 cubic feet should be enough. Find a spot in your backyard to begin collecting your organic waste. A shady spot is recommended, as is a place far enough away from your usual outside activity (hey, compost doesn't exactly smell like roses, although you can use it on your roses).

2. **Build your bin.** To make one out of wood, you don't need to be incredibly handy. Using scrap lumber or even new wood—but staying away from treated lumber—nail together a box big enough to collect what you'll compost. In some cases, you can even contain everything with chicken wire or another fencing material. Make sure to have one side that will allow easy access to the compost pile.

3. **Start adding organic matter.** Examples of what you can add: grass clippings, leaves, coffee grounds, eggshells, banana

peels, tea bags, shredded paper, dead plants. Examples of what NOT to add: meat scraps, sawdust, human or pet waste, diseased plants, pernicious weeds.

4. **Keep the pile ventilated and moist.** When starting out, make sure not to add too much of one thing. It could create clumps and prevent the necessary ventilation that allows the micro-organisms to break down all of the materials and turn it into healthy compost.

5. **Turn the pile—to allow air to circulate properly—at least every other week.** With your handy shovel or pitchfork, turn the pile by bringing the material on the inside to the outside and vice versa. This ensures that the entire pile has a chance to decompose.

6. **Spread it.** To tell if your pile is ready to spread throughout your garden, make sure it looks dark brown, feels crumbly, and smells earthy. You can spread a layer of your new compost up to one inch thick in your garden beds.

RESULTS:
> Trash kept out of landfills.
> Best soil nutrients money can't buy.
> Healthier earth.

recipe for revolution #4

SET UP A RAIN BARREL

If you've got a green thumb and want to save the earth while growing beautiful gardens, look to the clouds. They'll save you money and cut down on your water use if you're able to harvest the rain. After all, it's free, there's a lot of it, and it's nature's way of quenching thirst. Why would you use anything else to water your plants?

Did you know **that even though the earth is 2/3 water,**

only 3/10 of one percent is suitable for domestic use?[2]
And here we are dumping it on our plants. Flowers and
trees like rain; why not give them more of it?

INGREDIENTS:
> Large Plastic Barrel
> Short Hose for overflow water
> Flexible Down Sport
> Screwdriver
> Drill
> Hammer
> Mosquito Dunks (optional)
Approximate Cost: $75
Time: About 45 minutes

STEPS:
1. **Get your barrel.** Some cities offer these for free, but
if yours doesn't, you can find one online very easily. Check
auction sites for some great deals—especially cool are barrels
that used to be something else, so you keep trash out of a
landfill while you conserve water. (Some barrels also come with
their own sets of instructions.)

2. **Place your barrel on a flat surface, directly under a
downspout—which you may need to saw off to meet
the barrel's height—to maximize rain collection.** The
rain will come out of the downspout and enter into the barrel
from the top, through a set of holes.

3. **Attach the spigot.** Just like the faucet outside where your
hose connects, you'll use a spigot to get water from your barrel
to your watering can.

4. **Attach a run-off hose.** Because the barrel will fill quickly
(and you probably won't use all of the water in your barrel,
unless you live in a dry area), you may need to drill a hole for a
run-off hose.

5. **Wait for it to rain.** A rainfall of just an inch will provide enough water to fill a 75-gallon barrel, so after one spring shower, you will have all the water you'll need.

6. **Add mosquito dunks.** Even though most barrels will come with a mesh screen on the top to prevent mosquitoes from congregating, you can buy pellets to add to the water to make sure pests stay away all spring and summer.

RESULTS:
> Thousands of gallons of water saved.
> Conservation of natural resources.
> Happy and healthy plants.

a beginner's glossary

Still have questions about the language of revolution?
Peruse the list below to get some basic information about the
terms and ideas we use throughout the book.

501(c)(3): Specific designation of a nonprofit that is tax-exempt and
whose donations are tax-deductible (for the donor).

Biodegradable: Process by which something is able to decay
through living organisms.

Change agent: Usually synonymous with charity or nonprofit, this
term describes an organization (or individual) who seeks to change
society in some meaningful way.

Chip: The handsome pitchman for CoolPeopleCare. He has appeared
on stickers and shirts all over the country. Chip was designed by Jeff
Carroll from Robertson Design (robertsondesign.com).

CO2: Scientific shorthand for carbon dioxide. This is the by-product of
driving cars, burning coal, and exhaling. It's bad for the environment,

collecting in our atmosphere and trapping heat from escaping, resulting in a greenhouse effect. It's important to put out as little of this as possible.

Compact florescent light bulb (CFL): A light bulb that uses less energy to produce light.

E-mail signature: The automated closing of an e-mail. Many e-mail programs allow the user to insert contact information or anything else that will be added to the bottom of each e-mail sent, such as a phone number, address, or other relevant information.

Farmers' market: Place that allows the growers of plants and food to sell their good directly to the customer, instead of going through an intermediary like a grocery store.

Fair trade: Term used to describe goods that have been allowed to set a floor price, meaning a fair price has been paid for their value. This process allows the producers of these goods to earn their money fairly and provide for their families.

Five minutes: 1/12 of an hour. While a seemingly short amount of time, a lot of good can be accomplished in as little as five minutes.

Free range: Term used for animals that have been allowed to roam, instead of being caged, while being raised to produce meat products.

Fuel efficiency: How much gas you use to get you where you're going. Fuel-efficient cars are those that get the farthest per gallon. You should buy cars with high fuel efficiency. Also known as fuel economy.

Geothermal power: An energy system that uses the temperature of the earth for power.

Going green: Phrase used to describe actions and habits that help save the environment.

Incandescent light bulb: Traditional light bulb that produces both light and heat, resulting in wasted energy.

Keep coal in the ground: A term used to describe energy savings. Most of the electricity in the U.S. comes from coal; thus by using less electricity, the need for coal is also lessened, allowing it to be kept in the ground.

Kilowatt hour: How energy use is measured. On average, it takes one pound of coal to produce one kilowatt hour of energy.

Hybrid: Term used to describe a car that uses more than one form of energy to power the engine.

MySpace: One of the most popular social-networking sites.

Nonprofit: Term used to describe an organization that does not return a dividend to shareholders. Instead it spends all money it receives from donations and grants.

Organic: A word used to describe a product or process that meets a certain set of ethical and environmental guidelines.

Pesco-vegetarian: A vegetarian that does not eat any meat but fish.

Phantom loading: The power that transfers from the socket to something that is plugged in, even when it's not on or in use. This can result in higher energy bills as you are paying for electricity you're not even using.

Pesticides: Unnatural chemicals often used on plants to keep away pests.

Recycle: Chemical process by which waste material is converted to useable products.

Renewable energy: Energy that can be used to power our homes and offices from sources that won't be depleted by our using them, such as wind, sun, and water power.

Ridesharing: Also known as carpooling, this term describes the idea of not driving alone, thereby keeping cars off the road and CO2 out of the air.

Shade grown: Term used to describe that coffee production didn't happen via leveling forests in order to grow beans. Coffee grown in or near shade actually makes the bean grow better.

Social networking: The phenomenon by which people can connect to other people online. Many social networking Web sites have appeared in the last few years, allowing people to make online connections and form a "social network."

Vegan: Someone who doesn't eat or use products made from animals or animal by-products. Most vegans won't eat eggs or dairy products or use leather products.

Vegetarian: Someone who doesn't eat meat or products made with meat by-products. Some vegetarians will eat eggs and dairy products.

Volatile Organic Compound (VOC): A form of air pollution, usually recognized by a strong smell. Most paint and gasoline contain VOCs.

Waste: The unusable, end product of any thing or process. Also known as trash. Reducing waste is better for the environment, since most waste is good for absolutely nothing.

Wi-Fi: Term used to describe a wireless Internet connection, by which someone can get online and not have to physically connect a cable to their computer.

Wish list: Many nonprofits keep a running list of some of their needs, in addition to monetary donations and volunteers. Many wish list items are things we use everyday and easily can be picked up at your local grocery or retail store.

behind the numbers

Sometimes, numbers get batted around like a volleyball in sixth-grade gym class. Because we want you, a very cool person, to be informed enough to act, we're providing you with the reasons we thought that the stats and data we used were important.

CHAPTER 1

1: Only 60 percent of us work a traditional 9-to-5 job.
This comes from the article "Flexible schedules and shift work: replacing the '9-to-5' workday?" by Thomas M. Beers. Published in 2000 in *Monthly Labor Review*, this article is a very interesting read about how the way we work is changing. bls.gov/opub/mlr/2000/06/art3full.pdf

2: Annie Dillard wrote, "How we spend our days is how we spend our lives."
From page 32 in *The Writing Life*. If you haven't read this book, Sam highly suggests it, especially if you've ever wanted to write anything in your life.

3: 50 extra hours
For this estimate, we just used our awesome calculators. Check it out: nine minutes a day times 365 days equals 3,285 minutes or 54.75 hours.

4: you'll save about five gallons of water
This estimate is based on what a typical shower uses in the U.S. Review more typical usage charts as part of the Lifestyle Project of Skidmore College:
skidmore.edu/~jthomas/lifestyleproject/btuusagecharts.html

5: you'll save more than 1,825 gallons of water and $11 in utility costs
Again, that calculator came in handy.

6: $30 billion worth of organic products are sold each year in the United States
This statistic was found in the June 2005 "Organic, Inc." article in *San Francisco Chronicle* by Jason Mark exploring the mainstreaming of organics.
sfgate.com/cgi-bin/article.cgi?file=/chronicle/archive/2005/06/09/EDGISD5JL61.DTL

CHAPTER 2
1: The average American spends 100 hours each year just getting to their 40-hour-a week gig.
This fact is pretty overwhelming, given how precious our time is. The U.S. Census Bureau published this report:
census.gov/Press-Release/www/releases/archives/american_community_survey_acs/004489.html

2: with almost 300 million cars on the roads of North America

If you ask us, that's a lot of vehicles taking up a lot of asphalt and spewing out a lot of emissions. But you don't have to take our word for it; this is according to the Auto Channel:

theautochannel.com/news/2004/10/13/251312.html

3: 63 percent of people killed in accidents weren't wearing seatbelts

This is a fact that doesn't have to exist. Buckling up is so easy, but so many of us still don't do it.

car-accidents.com/pages/seat_belts.html

4: 75 percent of us still drive solo

We found this eye-opening number in a piece published in the June 14, 2007, *Orlando Sentinel*. It's a great article full of more eye-openers: "Commute is lonely—but options are limited" by Jay Hamburg and Sarah Langbein.

5: reduce gas mileage by up to 10 percent

We told you that *Orlando Sentinel* article was good. That's where we found this info as well.

6: nearly 33 percent of all traffic deaths are speed-related

Again, this is another statistic we hope becomes extinct. See Car and Driver for more information on this topic:

caranddriver.com/article.asp?section_id=30&article_id=9686

7: you could improve your fuel economy by nearly 10 percent

Vehicle-information guide Edmunds came out with a great

list of the top-10 ways you can improve your fuel economy.
edmunds.com/reviews/list/top10/103164/article.html

8. the average car emits nearly 125 grams of CO2 per mile
We found this minutia of car info on the Earth Trends Web
site:

earthtrends.wri.org/features/view_featurephp?theme+5&f
id=53

CHAPTER 3

1: We spend almost a third of our adult life working
For this bit of depressing information, we simply used our
reasoning powers: if you work for eight hours a day, that's a
third of your day. Granted you don't work that much every
day, but some folks do. And there's the overtime factor.

**2: Doing so will use 80 percent less electricity and cut
CO2 emissions by more than 500 pounds each year.**
We stumbled across this information at Consumer Reports'
Greener Choices site. There, you'll find more ways to cut
back on your emissions, especially lots of little, easy changes
(which we like, of course).
greenerchoices.org/globalwarmingathome.cfm

3: Americans recycle nearly half of all paper used
As a country, we're off to a good start, but we could be
recycling more. This piece from Paper University exposes
our laziness and motivates us to act:
tappi.org/paperu/all_about_paper/earth_answers/
Whyrec1.html

4: nearly 300 million empty printer and toner cartridges are dumped into landfills
That's a big number, and one that we can work to trim significantly. This idea was brought to our attention by Jeffrey Davis who writes weekly at *The Fun Times Guide to Living Green*.
green.thefuntimesguide.com/2007/06/ink_jet_printer_refills.php

CHAPTER 4
1: 108 million Americans who drinks coffee
We thought this statistic would be higher, but the truth remains that coffee is still one of the "it" drinks out there. And that's why we did a whole chapter on it. For more coffee-related information, visit E-Importz.com.
e-importz.com/Support/specialty_coffee.htm

2: with more than 25,000 coffeehouses in the U.S.
We thought this stat would be higher, too. The World Tea Expo has all of the facts for your, um, consumption.
worldteaexpo.com/index.php?option=com_content&task=view&id=66

3: With 75 percent of the world's coffee supply coming from small-scale farms
But this stat we didn't realize was so high. That doesn't diminish the need for every coffee consumer to drink fair trade so that all coffee growers can have a fair wage and great working conditions.
oxfamamerica.org/newsandpublications/press_releases/press_release.2006-04-05.5805265801

4: 500 million cups of coffee sold each day in the U.S.
That's a lot of java.
itfacts.biz/index.php?id=P5155

5: More than 44 billion paper cups are used each year for hot drinks.
Insulair announced these findings from the Food Service & Packaging Institute in their April 4, 2006, news release.

6: If you use your own mug every day this year, you'll save a tree all by yourself.
We didn't think this was possible until we read this article in *The Portland Mercury* by M. William Helfrich & Justin Wescoat Sanders:
portlandmercury.com/portland/Content?oid-29552&category-34029

CHAPTER 5
1: Seventy percent of Americans use the Internet.
This number will only increase as it becomes easier to get online. As you might expect, a site called Internet World Stats keeps up with information like this:
internetworldstats.com/stats2.htm

2. triple the amount that used it just 10 years ago
This is also from Internet World Stats.

3: The average person spends 48 percent of their free time online.
Again, this stat from the Center for Media Research should only increase as more and more fun things happen digitally.
mediapost.com/research/cfmr_briefArchive.cfm?s=60649

4: the average person spends more time online than watching television

This information has far-reaching implications for our understanding of media and how it's used. Read Rob McGann's article, "Internet Edges Out Family Time More Than TV Time" for more information.

clickz.com/showPage.html?page=3455061

5: there are now over 60 million of them

Blogs are growing rapidly, as people learn just how easy it is to write about things that are important to them. If you want more detailed stats on blogs, bloggers, and blogging, visit Blog Herald:

blogherald.com/2005/05/25/world-wide-blog-count-for-may-now-over-60-million-blogs/

CHAPTER 6

1: Americans spend more than $1.3 billion every day eating out.

That's a lot of money. And a lot of food. See what else you can dig up on Answers.com, which is where we found this snapshot of the food industry:

answers.com/topic/eating-places?cat-biz-fin

2: over 800,000 restaurants in the U.S.

Like we said, that industry snapshot was full of great data:

answers.com/topic/eating-places?cat-biz-fin

3: The average American child produces 67 pounds of trash a year just from their lunch.
We were alerted of the massive amount of waste we all produce at lunchtime by WasteFreeLunches.
wastefreelunches.org

4: you'll save about $1 and keep two pounds of coal in the ground
If you want to know how much electricity your appliances use (and therefore how much money and coal you'll save by not using them), check out Mr. Electricity's article on "How to save energy when you cook."
michaelbluejay.com/electricity/cooking.html

5: Frozen food requires 10 times more energy to produce than fresh food
This is one of the best reasons for eating local, organic food. Not only will you be healthier, but so will the planet. See tip #28 at the Global Warming Facts Web site:
globalwarming-facts.info/50-tips.html

6: the average household throwing away more than 470 pounds of food each year
That's a lot of wasted food.
acfnewsource.org/science/garbage_galore.html

7: one of the 2.2 million people who call themselves a waiter or waitress
The U.S. Department of Labor keeps all kind of information on how we work.
bls.gov/oco/ocos162.htm

8: Fewer than 20 percent of us don't eat meat.

Even though this statistic is low, more and more people are becoming vegetarians or even going vegan. The Vegetarian Resource Group has lots of information about the topic. vrg.org/nutshell/poll.htm

9: If everyone in the U.S. ate one locally produced, organic, vegetarian meal each week, we'd save one million barrels of oil.

This wonderful statistic is found on page 5 of Barbara Kingsolver's book *Animal, Vegetable, Miracle*, which Sam's wife, Lynnette, highly recommends.

CHAPTER 7

1: 500 billion plastic grocery bags are consumed worldwide each year.

This is a huge number and, like most huge numbers, it may be hard to get our head around it. We found this information in the *National Geographic* article "Are Plastic Grocery Bags Sacking the Environment?" by John Roach (September 2, 2003).

CHAPTER 8

1: Although Americans make up only five percent of the world's population, we use 26 percent of its energy.

Something doesn't seem quite equitable about this. Look up more daunting facts at Solar Energy International.

solarenergy.org/resources/energyfacts.html

2: The average American family spends $1,900 a year on energy.
What a pain in the pocket. This is the national average, according to the U.S. Environmental Protection Agency. Of course, doing all of the things we suggest in this book will help you lower what you owe.
fypower.org/news/?p-363

3. the average household uses 450 pounds of coal a year
We did the math on this one. Phantom loading uses between two and eight percent of your total electricity (rochsolartech. itcstore.com/default.aspx?p=111422). The average house uses about 12,500 kWh (and pounds of coal) a year.

4: If every American household changed their five most-used light fixtures from regular light bulbs to energy-saving incandescent bulbs, the energy savings would be the equivalent of taking eight million cars off the road, saving $6 billion in energy costs for the nation!
This statement is proof that if all of us do the small things needed to make the world a better place, our collective action will add up to make a big difference.
topbulb.com/energystar/

5: you can save up to $5 and keep about 10 pounds of coal in the ground
We did a little math here, based on a chart put out by *Seattle City Light*, which allows you to see how much electricity each appliances in your house uses:
ci.seattle.wa.us/light/accounts/stretchyourdollar/ac5_appl.htm#Laundry

CHAPTER 9

1: your yearly trash production of more than 1,500 pounds
This is a lot of garbage. That's all we have to say about that. Any reduction we can make in our personal waste is well worth it.
wiki.answers.com/Q/How_much_garbage_do_humans_make_a_year

2. average American receives about 500 pieces of junk mail every year, weighing nearly 30 pounds
According to the State of New Hampshire, junk mail is a major source of waste, and one that's easy to correct.
des.state.nh.us/JunkMail/

3: over one billion people around the world in need of glasses
Unite for Sight, Inc. knows the need for glasses around the world is great, and provides your used glasses to people who need to see.
uniteforsight.org/donate_eyeglasses.php

4: Americans spending $17 billion on paint each year
The Worldwatch Institute keeps tabs on ways to make our world more sustainable. We found all of our information about paint there.
worldwatch.org/node/1496

5: Americans throw away enough aluminum every three months to rebuild our entire commercial airline fleet.
If you ever wondered if recycling made that much of a difference, this statistic says it all. Tossing a can in the recycling bin (rather than the garbage can) is an easy way to save precious resources.
sandiegozoo.org/society/critters.html

6. Recycling a four-foot stack of newspapers saves a 40-foot tree.

Like cans, newspapers are easy to recycle, and make an important difference in our world. If you haven't already, get some recycling bins for your house and collect paper to be recycled.

oroloma.org/resources/kidscorner/earthday/2005/recyclingFacts.html

7: Every glass bottle recycled saves enough energy to power a 100-watt light bulb for four hours.

The San Diego County Office of Education figured this one out.

littercleanup.tripod.com/recycle.id9.html

8: In the United States, 63,000 garbage trucks are filled every single day.

We throw away a lot of stuff. Properly recycling what we could would decrease this statistic.

cqc.com/~ccswmd/trivia.htm

9: U.S. waste per capita has more than doubled in the past 40 years from 2.5 pounds per person per day to nearly five pounds a day.

10: Only two percent of all waste is municipal solid waste. The rest is industrial. Even if we could eliminate all of our household trash through recycling, reusing, and composting, 98 percent of all trash would still exist, just to make the stuff we use."

11: By reusing a sofa, you'll keep the 100-pound sofa out of a landfill, and you'll also keep as much as 20 times

that in raw materials from being used.
Deron Beal, the founder of Freecycle™, let us in on these
three statistics. He has spent the last four years developing
Freecycle™ and is a wealth of information regarding the
way we use things and how we can keep from throwing lots
of stuff away.

CHAPTER 10

**1: more than 25 million people in the U.S. suffering
from poor diets**
To address the vast amount of people with poor diets,
Garden Writers have undertaken the Plant a Row initiative,
which is where we learned just how many people suffer
from malnutrition.
gardenwriters.org/par

**2: The average child spends 1,680 minutes each week
watching TV.**
That's a lot of TV. And, as we mentioned earlier, it will soon
be a lot of Internet time. But the point of this suggestion
is to get kids (and adults) off of the computers and couches
and interact with one another. We got this data from The
Sourcebook for Teaching Science.
csun.edu/science/health/docs/tv&health.html

CHAPTER 11

1: who will collectively spend nearly half a trillion dollars
The National Retail Federation keeps up with what we're
all spending and on what:
nrf.com/content/default.asp?folder=press/release2006&f
ile=holidayforecast0906.htm&bhcp=1

2: the average person spends nearly $1,000 each December
The American Research Group did the math on what we
spend individually around the holidays:
americanresearchgroup.com/holiday

**3: In 2006 holiday donations enabled the Salvation Army
to assist 34 million people.**
For more information about the good work the Salvation Army
does with your holiday donations, visit ringbells.org.

**4. it uses 44 percent less energy to create while reducing
greenhouse emissions by 37 percent**
The Sierra Club provided this motivating statistic.

RECIPES FOR REVOLUTION
**1: Most sinks use 3 to 4 gallons of water per minute,
though the government put in place regulations for any
faucet made after 1994, mandating no more than 2.2
gallons per minute of flow.**
This site has even more statistics and details on installing
faucet aerators.
peninsulacool.wetpaint.com/page/Challenge%3A+Install
+Faucet+Aerators

**2: that even though the earth is 2/3 water, only 3/10 of
one percent is suitable for domestic use**
This site has everything you'd ever need to know about rain
barrels. If we haven't convinced you that you need one for
your garden, it surely will.
rainbarrelguide.com/

coolpeoplecare:
how it all started

We tell people that this whole thing started in less than five minutes. That's sort of true. While we didn't initiate the concept, build the site, launch the revolution, and keep it all going in less than five minutes, the wheels did get turning pretty quickly.

We had been working in the nonprofit world for a while and saw how quickly things were changing. The way money was raised, volunteers were recruited, awareness was spread, and time was spent in the charitable world was being transformed.

But we still came into contact with countless individuals who wanted to make a difference and didn't know how. Some wanted to raise awareness, some wanted to get their hands dirty, and others wanted to just fight the good fight of social change.

So there was a desire of people wanting to make a difference. And there was a need for these people by the organizations already doing so.

We wanted to help these two entities find each other. The best way to make that happen was by creating an online resource, a destination, where these two could learn about each other, make a meaningful connection, and save the world in the process.

And CoolPeopleCare was born.

Whenever we'd talk to people about why they didn't care (and therefore, weren't cool), we got two excuses:

> I don't know how.

> I don't have enough time.

We figured that if we could eliminate these two excuses, we could serve as a catalyst to inspire social change like never before. By daring people to start small and become passionate about something, we'd have a social revolution as more and more people pitched in, got involved, and helped out.

And so we created a Web site. People are online. That's where we meet them. Nonprofits need to be online to meet these people who want to give back. That's what we give them.

We want people to go online, come to us, get their idea for how to save the world today, and then log off, shut down their computer, leave their house, and make it happen. We want to push folks out of their homes and comfort zones and into situations that badly need them.

Our ultimate goal is to be THE online resource for anyone who wants to make a difference. If that means that you do so in a few minutes a day at home with your kids, then we've got those ideas. And if that means you spend a few hours every weekend volunteering somewhere, we've got those opportunities as well.

We'll be your destination for ideas by showing you other destinations for action.

When a new day dawns, we are all given the same amount of time to use as we wish. we will have a chance to erase the slate clean of yesterday's mistakes and lay foundations for tomorrow's success. And so we can pander to the status quo, or work for the common good; we can focus on the bottom line or on one in need; we can chase every dollar, or follow where hope will lead us. Because at the end of the day, what will distinguish us will be what we gave, how we served, and who we loved.

by sam davidson & stephen schuyler
www.coolpeoplecare.org

ACKNOWLEDGEMENTS

No one gets where they're going alone. Even if they set out and show up solo, there have been people in their past or present who helped in some way. As we journey through life, it is important to pause and offer gratitude to those who have given of their presence, advice, or trust in meaningful ways.

This is our attempt to honor those who helped us get this far:

To Malinda Moseley and Lynnette Davidson. Without the love and support from our wives, there isn't much we'd be able to accomplish. Thanks for letting us take the risk that has been CoolPeopleCare thus far, and for standing beside us throughout.

To our friends and family who have provided valuable insight when we've needed it most. We especially want to thank our advisory board and staff: Jen Cole, Steve Davidson, Leslye Stewart Ford, Thomas Kleinert, Betsy Neely, Leigh Piper, Beth Richardson, Zack Samples, Jeff Simmons, Adam Solesby, Jim Stewart, Helen Trabue, and Anderson Williams.

To the kind people at Oasis Center, who believed in us and allowed us the space and opportunity to dream and try to new things. Each person there is special and does incredibly meaningful work. We especially want to thank Hal Cato, Jane Fleishman, and Bette Schulman.

To each and every one of our nonprofit partners. Your willingness to take a risk in us pushed us to dream even bigger:

CHEEKWOOD

CHILDREN ARE PEOPLE, INC.

CIVIC DESIGN CENTER

GENERATION TENNESSEE

GIVING MATTERS

GOVERNOR'S BOOKS FROM BIRTH FOUNDATION

HANDS ON NASHVILLE

HOSPITAL HOSPITALITY HOUSE

THE JASON FOUNDATION

LIONSHARE LEADERSHIP GROUP

MOTHERS AGAINST DRUNK DRIVING *(Tennessee Chapter)*

NAMI — TN

OASIS CENTER

PARK CENTER

ROCKETOWN

ROLLING HILLS COMMUNITY CHURCH

RONALD MCDONALD HOUSE – CHATTANOOGA

SCARRITT BENNETT CENTER

SPORTS 4 ALL FOUNDATION

TENNESSEE DISABILITY COALITION

TENNESSEE FOREIGN LANGUAGE INSTITUTE

TENNESSEE IMMIGRANT AND REFUGEE RIGHTS COALITION

THE TMA GROUP

THE TOMORROW FUND

UNITED WAY OF METROPOLITAN NASHVILLE

VINE STREET CHRISTIAN CHURCH

And to each and every one of the cool people out there. Thanks for visiting our site, daring to make a difference, and participating in the 5 Minute Revolution. The world is better because you're in it.

about the
authors

SAM DAVIDSON is the co-founder and president of CoolPeopleCare, Inc. Telling the stories that need telling in order to motivate others to change the things that need changing, Sam is a social entrepreneur who believes in the power of local communities. Having worked and consulted in the nonprofit arena, his approach to impacting one's world is believable and, even more importantly, doable.

STEPHEN MOSELEY is the co-founder and vice president of CoolPeopleCare, Inc. As a communications consultant and design professional focusing on the work of nonprofits, Stephen has worked to build brands through meaningful connections while empowering hard-working organizations to control their message and mission through the creative and efficient use of technology.

Authors photographed by Rob Williams

about the
fonts

Imperfect

This font is used in the heads and folios of this book and was designed by Mike Strassburger. Mr. Strassburger also designed the font "Arrowmatic." While unintentional, this font's use in *New Day Revolution* is nothing short of serendipitous. In truth, we are all imperfect. And with a constant understanding of this undeniable fact, we all have an opportunity to push forward, grow stronger, and be better. We hope this book serves as a guide and inspiration to do all three.

Mrs. Eaves

This font is used for the body copy in this book and was designed by Zuzana Licko. Mrs. Licko also designed the popular fonts "Journal" and "Tarzana." The authors of this book don't know a Mrs. Eaves. They never had a teacher named Mrs. Eaves. There are few last names that even rhyme with "Eaves" and, as such, they know of no direct or indirect connection between the font named "Mrs. Eaves" and this book. Other than it is a lovely serif font.